D0563701

WITHDRAWN FROM
MACALESTER COLLEGE
LIBRARY

The Long Struggle

WELL-FUNCTIONING
WORKING-CLASS
BLACK FAMILIES

The Long Struggle

WELL-FUNCTIONING WORKING-CLASS BLACK FAMILIES

Jerry M. Lewis, M.D.

Director of Research, Timberlawn Psychiatric Research Foundation;
Psychiatrist-in-Chief, Timberlawn Psychiatric Hospital;
Clinical Professor of Psychiatry and Family Practice and
Community Medicine, Southwestern Medical School of the
University of Texas at Dallas

and

John G. Looney, M.D.

Research Psychiatrist, Timberlawn Psychiatric Research Foundation;
Staff Psychiatrist, Timberlawn Psychiatric Hospital

BRUNNER/MAZEL, *Publishers* • New York

Library of Congress Cataloging in Publication Data

Lewis, Jerry M., 1924–
  The long struggle.

  Includes bibliographical references and index.
  1. Afro-American families.   2. Afro-Americans—
Psychology.   I. Looney, John G., 1941–   . II. Title.
[DNLM: 1. Blacks.   2. Family.   3. Interpersonal
relations.   4. Mental health.   5. Social class.   WA
305 L6741]
E185.86.L48   1983   306.8′08996073   83-14361
ISBN 0-87630-342-4

Copyright © 1983 by Jerry M. Lewis and John Looney

Published by

BRUNNER/MAZEL, INC.
19 Union Square West
New York, New York 10003

No part of this book may be reproduced by any process whatsoever without the written permis-
sion of the copyright owner.

MANUFACTURED IN THE UNITED STATES OF AMERICA

To Pat and Susan for their remarkable support,
understanding, and love.

Contents

Acknowledgments

The research described in this book was supported, in part, by grants from The Trull Foundation of Palacious, Texas, and Robert B. Trull. Without their interest in lower-income, minority families, the project would not have been initiated. The two grants were in the form of challenges to the Board of Trustees of the Timberlawn Psychiatric Research Foundation to raise matching funds. The Trustees responded quickly and, as before and since, were led by the energy and generosity of Charles and Sarah Seay. Many Trustees participated in the successful effort to match the initial grants, and we are particularly indebted to the leadership provided by two individuals, James M. Moroney, Jr., and David L. Florence, successive Chairmen of the Board of Trustees.

Additional funding which became necessary in the final stages of the data analysis and manuscript preparation was provided by income from three funds within the Timberlawn Psychiatric Research Foundation Endowment. These were the Sarah and Charles E. Seay Fund, the Samuel Roberts Noble Fund, and the Crystal Charity Ball Fund.

The research project was accomplished by a group of professionals, some of whom are long-time members of the research team and others who joined the team specifically for this project. In the former group, John T. Gossett, Ph.D., Associate Director of the Foundation, and Virginia Austin Phillips, Senior Research Associate, provided essential help in all areas of the research and manuscript preparation. F. David Barnhart, M.A., provided methodological assistance and statistical analyses which were invaluable. In the latter group, Charles B. Thomas, Ph.D., provided insights regarding black families and contributed particularly to the exploration of family values. Carolyn Meador, R.N., located the families, encouraged them to participate and assisted in gathering data. Truman E. Thomas, M.S., the West Dallas Youth Clinic, not only knew the neighborhood, but was actively involved in gathering data. Other professionals and graduate students who were involved in rating family tapes included Cynthia Lewis Riedel, Betty J. Feemster, M.S.W., and Richard A. Mallard, Ph.D. Nannette Bruchey was her usual indefatigable self in preparing the manuscript. To all these colleagues we are most grateful.

Our clinical colleagues at the Timberlawn Psychiatric Hospital supported the project enthusiastically. In particular we wish to thank Doyle I. Carson, M.D., Medical Director, and Keith H. Johansen, M.D., Director of Professional Education.

This study expanded our base of operations to new neighborhoods in which we were strangers. A number of agencies and individuals made our acceptance possible, and we wish to thank them. Drew W. Alexander, M.D., and John C. Edlin, M.D., successive Directors of the West Dallas Youth Clinic, and their entire staff provided insights into the implementation of the study and introduced the research team to the West Dallas black community. A number of pastors representing several ministerial alliances in the black community accepted the validity of our intentions and introduced us to families who participated in the study. Joseph L. Honore, principal of Pinkston High School, and the Student Council of that school "adopted" the project and helped to locate families.

At a more personal level, both the collection of data and the preparation of the manuscript required time usually spent with our families, and we appreciate their tolerance of our frequent unavailability.

Finally, we wish to thank the participating families. Most of them had severely limited economic resources, despite which they gave their time and trust with remarkable generosity. We hope that they will conclude that their involvement in the project was worthwhile.

Jerry M. Lewis, M.D.
John G. Looney, M.D.
March, 1983

The Long Struggle

WELL-FUNCTIONING
WORKING-CLASS
BLACK FAMILIES

CHAPTER 1

In the Beginning

". . . I mean, we don't have any problems or anything. Now, we have had problems up to this present time. We've had . . . we've had problems. But we worked them out. One thing about married life, you've got to want it. See. Take a lot of marriages, they'll stay married for three, four, or five years and oh, they start thinking only about themselves. When you get that way, you can't, your marriage is not, you won't be successful because you're only thinking about yourself. Got to think about more than yourself when you're married. 'Cause when you make that vow to live with that person the rest of your life that's important. Actually, you're saying, I'm gonna share my happiness and so forth with you, and we're in this together, you know. A lot of young people, they'll get married for a little while then say, 'I'll get me a divorce.' Divorce is easy to get now if you got a little money (laughs). I think if divorces were harder to get, more would stay together. Kinda force them, in a sense of speaking, to stay you know.

"But we don't have any problems. Oh, we could, we could. I'd like to have a new car or something like that, you know, something. It's always you're gonna *want* something. I think that's the way life is."

1

This simple, yet eloquent, statement came from the father in one of the black, working-class families that are the focus of this book. The statement came at the end of a lengthy exploratory interview in answer to the final question, "Is there anything else that would help us to understand you and your family better?" The interview was conducted at the family home, a small frame house located on a short street near a major traffic artery. The house was sorely in need of repair and paint. The yard, more mud than grass, was littered with tires, decomposed mattresses, and rusted toys.

The interior of the 900 square foot house was clean, sparsely furnished and, on this May day in Texas, very hot. The father was proud of his home — in particular, the fact that they were buying instead of renting. He is a construction foreman, and his wife is a domestic servant. Their combined annual income is $12,500. With this income they are raising four children (one boy and three girls, ages 15, 14, 11, and six). Money is often a problem, and the absence of any reserves is graphically illustrated by the following segment of an exploratory interview with his wife, who was asked about "bad times" in the marriage.

"Well, like, he had his back broken when my baby, next to the baby girl, Nancy, was about a year old. He was in a car wreck, and he was down for about a year, but I don't really think that was a bad time. Even though, see, I would go to the hospital and see him every day. I worked three days then, but the Welfare Department, the State, they helped us, and we kept our bills paid up. When I look back on it, I don't really think it was a bad time. You know, we still had our needs, and we had everything paid, our rent, and we kept everything going, but we didn't get anything else. We didn't expect to get our *wants* because at that time he wasn't able to work and I only worked three days so they gave us what we needed. Well, I mean, we, they supplied our *needs* and I worked three days and they let me work and I went to see him every day so it wasn't really a bad time. 'Cause you know, times be worse at that time, but then it's gone and then you look back at it, and then you say, 'Well, I was really blessed in a way because he's still, you know, he was not paralyzed.' The doctor said that he was lucky he wasn't paralyzed. And he was lucky that he wasn't dead. So I was really blessed and I was really thankful for that. Everybody cooperated. My mother-in-law kept the kids and I went to see him every day after work, you know. Days I didn't work, I went to see him in the morning, and the days I did work I went to see him in the afternoon. So it was kind of rough without him being here, but I don't guess it was really a bad time."

When this family was together for interviews or interactional testing, they demonstrated a great deal of warmth and humor. Family members listened carefully to each other and obviously respected each other's opinions. When asked to solve experimental problems, the parents shared leadership, encouraged the children's participation, and negotiated solutions. There was no suggestion of underlying chronic conflict; the family functioned smoothly as a group.

These and other family characteristics are associated with high levels of family competence or psychological health as identified in our previous work with middle- and upper-middle-class, white families. The families studied earlier, however, lived in a very different socioeconomic world: They lived in affluent suburban neighborhoods, owned several cars, and anticipated college education for their children as a matter of course. Clearly, they had all their needs and most of their "wants."

This book reports our research group's initial study of a different social context, the inner city. Our primary interest is the impact of social context on family competence as revealed in family structure and function. There are numerous questions to express this interest: "How does being black and living in marginal economic circumstances affect what is possible in family life?" "How do economic and ethnic forces shape the structure and function of the family?" "How do some families manage to do very well despite a harsh environment?"

These are the kinds of questions that, in the beginning, moved our research group's base of operations to working-class, black neighborhoods. This book reports what we found focusing on families who appear to function well or, in different language, are healthy or competent.

FAMILY COMPETENCE

Family competence, as we use the term, describes the quality of possessing attributes necessary or helpful to achieve or accomplish given tasks. At the most basic level, of course, is the family's task of assuring the physical survival of its members. The matter of defining the subsequent tasks introduces complexity: We focus upon the tasks the family accomplishes for its individual members rather than the tasks the family does for the culture. We ask, "What does a psychologically healthy family, as a small social system, do for its members?"

Selection of the tasks is based on value judgments of the researchers using the term "competence." When the values upon which competence is to be evaluated are made explicit, readers may then agree or disagree with those values. This issue has become more complex for us over the years of involvement in family research. We began with Parsons' concept of two cardinal tasks: A family "ought" to raise children who become autonomous, and it "should" provide sufficient emotional support for stabilizing the parents' personalities and continuing their emotional maturation.[1] To the extent a family accomplishes the tasks, it can be considered competent; to the extent it fails at one or both tasks, it can be considered less competent or dysfunctional.

More recently, it has become apparent that a family "ought" to function in a way that provides family members with a balance of separateness and attachment consistent with the greatest probability of individual family members' adaptive success at different phases of life. Small children, for example, need a balance skewed in the direction of secure attachment, whereas young adult family members need a balance which emphasizes separateness. In this regard, separateness refers to more than the ability to experience one's self as a distinct or differentiated person. It includes higher order processes such as the capacity for autonomous functioning and, ultimately, the assumption of responsibility for one's own life. In the same sense, attachment means more than just the ability to relate. It involves the concepts of commitment and intimacy.

These overarching tasks of the family operate throughout the lifespan of the family. There are, in addition, family tasks of a different order that are associated with specific developmental stages in the life of the family. These stage-specific family tasks also represent value judgments. During the family's developmental stage of "early marriage," for example, we suggest that the competence of the couple's evolving relationship may be assessed by measuring the extent to which they accomplish three stage-specific tasks: 1) separating from parents of origin and emotionally investing in their own relationship (a task that can be understood from both the perspectives of transferring loyalty and of differentiating as a couple); 2) working out a mutually satisfactory distribution of power within their marital relationship; and 3) evolving a mutually satisfactory level of psychological intimacy within their relationship.

Because the family functions within a broader matrix of social, cultural, and economic systems that have an impact upon the family and to which the family contributes, contextual factors need careful consideration. Although the relationship between the family and the larger systems in which it is embedded is reciprocal, often the impact of the larger systems is greater. When, for example, a family lives in a disintegrating, violent neighborhood, it may (or may not) contribute to the social chaos, but it is certain to be affected, if only by developing a heightened sense of watchfulness and caution.

In the selection of family tasks upon which competence is to be evaluated, the role of contextual factors needs careful consideration. This ecological matrix includes a broad array of variables, such as economic factors, population density, the physical environment, cultural mores, social traditions, the rate of social change, and the level of integration or disintegration in the broader social system. The tasks upon which competence is to be judged are based upon what is possible under a given set of circumstances. The fact that, given any set of ecological circumstances, there is considerable variation in how different families manage is not, we believe, evidence for the unimportance of ecological factors. Rather, it speaks to the importance of including the construct of competence in understanding a particular family's way of dealing with social reality. We emphasize this position because, too often it seems, observers of different persuasions will either explain away high levels of competence in harsh circumstances or suggest that comparable levels are possible for all.

Once the family tasks are selected, it is possible to construct a Continuum of Family Competence. This is a dimensional approach to the development of a taxonomy and is a useful way of bringing order to a large and complex body of data. It is based on the assumption that the phenomena under study can best be understood as continuous rather than discontinuous. The assumption of discontinuity is best illustrated by the syndromic approach to classification, another approach to taxonomy. The American Psychiatric Association's *Diagnostic and Statistical Manual*, Third Edition,[2] for example, is essentially a syndromic or discontinuous classification of individual psychiatric disorders with the addition of two Axes (IV, V) which introduce a dimensional component. The dimensional approach to individual psychiatric disorders is illustrated by Luborsky's Health-Sickness Continuum.[3] In this approach to classification, psychiatric disorders are differentiated on the basis of a single, continuous variable.

Our earlier work resulted in the construction of a Continuum of Family Competence based on Parsons' two cardinal tasks: producing autonomous children and supporting stabilization and maturation of parental personalities. These tasks appear to have particular relevance for our sample of families with adolescent children because the children are nearing a period of life in which the demands for separateness will be accentuated and the parents are approaching a life stage (the "empty nest") in which there may be special needs for attachment to each other.

It was possible to locate both clinical and research volunteer families on this continuum and to demonstrate that at any point on the continuum there were striking similarities among families. Those families, for example, who accomplished well the two cardinal tasks were alike in many respects. Next on the continuum were families called "competent but pained" who were similar structurally and were raising autonomous children but doing less well at providing parental support. Dysfunctional families were characterized by rigidity, of either the dominant-submissive or chronically conflicted type. Severely dysfunctional families failed for the most part at both family tasks and often were enmeshed and chaotic. The Continuum of Family Competence will be described in detail in Chapter 2, but here we emphasize the general characteristics of the different family structures: most competent families — flexibility; dysfunctional families — rigidity; and severely dysfunctional families — chaos. The continuum, then, moves from flexibility →

rigidity→ chaos. It is also important to note that evidence suggests that, under circumstances of sufficient stress, a family's adaptive capacity can be overwhelmed, and the structure of the family may change. The structural change in a family also moves in the direction of flexibility→ rigidity→ chaos. Healing or reintegration of a family follows the reverse path of structural change; that is, from chaos→ rigidity→ flexibility. These issues are introduced at this point because they are relevant to an understanding of the development of this study of working-class, black families.

We have found significant clinical advantages to this conceptual scheme, and our previously reported data are strongly supportive.[4] At the present time, however, there is no broadly accepted family taxonomy; rather, there is a profusion of conceptual approaches, often reflecting the orientation of a particular research or clinical group or that of a particularly charismatic leader in the field. We believe this to be an essentially healthy state of affairs for a young discipline. There are few systematic studies in the field and as yet no consensus around any one conceptual scheme or model of family functioning. Our concept of family competence (itself not original) and the Continuum of Family Competence are offered as but one approach. In the final analysis a conceptual approach must be measured by the extent to which it both is useful in clinical endeavors and leads to important research questions, the answers to which may advance knowledge in the field.

We have found the continuum of competence to be a useful orienting structure clinically because it allows the identification of a structural pattern, which has implications for the nature of the clinician's interventions. The early recognition of chaotic, rigid, or flexible family structural patterns provides the clinician with an initial orientation around which to consider specific interventions tailored to the specific structure of the family. For example, the early recognition that the family structure is chaotic might lead the clinician to consider an authoritarian approach, by which some order may develop as a result of the clinician's "parenting" activities. A basically competent, flexible family coming to the clinician as the result of an acute stress might be helped best by collaborative support rather than the authoritarian mode, which might prove not only ineffective but harmful.

We would emphasize, however, that we consider locating a family on the Continuum of Family Competence to be an initial orienting and macroscopic clinical procedure. We would expect additional clinical data would help the clinician to understand better the ways in which families at any one point of the continuum and of similar overall competence are different.

The second measure of a conceptual scheme or model is the nature of the research questions that can be generated from it. We believe this study of working-class, black families offers examples of the kinds of questions that are possible.

THE EVOLUTION OF THE RESEARCH PROJECT

To most of its practitioners, clinical research with human subjects is not as rigorous a business as they might wish it to be. The focus on people introduces variations that cannot be completely controlled. The researcher articulates a hypothesis, identifies the instruments with which to measure the phenomena to be studied, locates and obtains the co-operation of a sample, and collects data. At each stage of the process, a number of questions must be answered. Some of these are fully anticipated, but others come as a surprise. At times it may not be possible to follow the original research design — and the project may be recast in terms of questions that are more answerable than those originally asked.

This study of working-class black families illustrates both the problems and the benefits of clinical research, and it may be useful to trace the development of the project for the reader. As a research team we had spent a number of years studying family structure and functioning of well-functioning middle-class families.[4] Our interest grew out of our research in treatment outcome and, specifically, the wish to know how family factors influenced treatment outcome in disturbed, hospitalized adolescents.[5] Studying the families of those adolescents required a control group of families containing adolescents. Within the group of control families, a cohort was identified that seemed unusually warm, responsive, and effective. Our interest in these families led to the development of the Healthy Family Project. Data from families from both the Treatment Outcome Project and the Healthy Family Project were used in constructing the Continuum of Family Competence.

Scientific presentations, seminars, and public addresses reporting our findings were met with expressed interest in both the conceptual model of the continuum of competence and the substantive findings from the study of well-functioning or healthy families. The presentations led to a number of requests from the mental health and medical communities for training in the use of the Beavers-Timberlawn Family Rating Scales.* These 13 scales were constructed to measure variables theoretically useful in measuring family competence. They cover a broad range of family processes and are evaluated by observing the whole family's involvement in experimental problem-solving.

Our findings had all the advantages of homogeneity and all the disadvantages of narrowness. We were asked repeatedly about the applicability of the findings to kinds of families different from those from whom the data were obtained. With few exceptions our sample was comprised of white, middle- and upper-middle-class, biologically intact, two-parent families with adolescent children. Questions involved such issues as lower-income families, ethnic minority families, single-parent families, recombined or stepfamilies, and families at other stages of family development, such as, for example, families with preschool children. Clearly, further research was needed to be able to answer these questions.

Out of these concerns a plan evolved to replicate our earlier work with a sample of lower-income families. Three groups of such families were present and potentially available — white, black, and Mexican-American. Our initial design called for the study of 20 families from each ethnic group. The selection of this number was based on the large amount of information collected from each family and its individual members and our hope to obtain sufficient funding to study 60 families in depth.

Initially two major hypotheses were articulated. The first hypothesis was that the three ethnic groups of families would be more alike than different if under the same degree of economic stress.

The second hypothesis was that, under the socioeconomic pressures to which such families were exposed, the most competent families would not manifest the flexible structure and effective functioning

---

*See Appendix A

noted in the previously studied white, middle- and upper-middle-class families. Rather they would demonstrate a pattern of moderate to marked dominance and submission. In other words, we predicted that, in this sample, the better functioning and most autonomous children and adults would come from dominant-submissive families, and that flexible families either would not be found in the sample or would be represented by only a few families. Stated in a different way, we predicted that, under the impact of economic stress, flexibility would not be adaptive and that more rigid family structures would be more suited to that context.

We were unable to find sufficient funding to pursue our original design. At length, partial funding was obtained and we decided to study 20 families from one ethnic group, hoping that additional funding would become available as the work progressed. The funding foundation preferred that we study an ethnic minority, and we decided to study black families both because there was a greater pool of full- and part-time black professionals from which to recruit research personnel and because with Mexican-American families we would introduce the complexity of a second language, Spanish, which was often spoken in the home. This might pose difficulties for the judges rating the videotapes of family interactional testing and exploratory family interviews.

Having decided to study intensively a small sample of poor black families with a particular focus on patterns of competence, we recruited the necessary research personnel, trained them in the use of our instruments, and sought to locate a suitable sample of families. In order to study a sample of families in some ways comparable to the previously studied middle- and upper-middle-class families, we restricted entry into the project to biologically intact, two-parent families. We did not anticipate the havoc that would bring to the process of locating a sample. The plan was to find intact families with adolescent children whose total family income was beneath the national poverty level. Such families do, of course, exist (and eventually there were several in our sample), but we found that most families at that income level were single-parent, mother-led families. It seemed that locating 20 intact families with incomes below the poverty level in our community and obtaining their cooperation would consume the entire two years for which we had funding. As a consequence, we relaxed the economic criteria for inclusion. This compromise resulted in a sample of working-class families. The data appear in Chapter 5, and the reader can judge whether these families can be considered "poor."

This compromise changed the focus of the study, and this change had both advantages and disadvantages. A major disadvantage is that by relaxing the income criterion we have presumably diminished or altered the stress. There may be, for example, a threshold effect for income below which the social stress is either quantitatively or qualitatively different.

An advantage to the change is that we can learn something of the characteristics of families that resist disintegration and the entry of their members to what has recently been termed the "underclass."[6] Although a more thorough understanding of that complexity awaits the insights derived from longitudinal studies of families, we believe our data offer preliminary clues as to the family characteristics that may be crucial.

At this point it is important to describe the hypotheses that, following these changes in the sample and research design, our study was designed to test.

The first hypothesis was that in a sample of intact, working-class black families there would be considerable diversity in structure and function.

The second hypothesis was that the working-class black families that best accomplished the two cardinal tasks of the family would demonstrate a rigid family structure of the dominant-submissive type and that the wife-mother would more often be the more dominant parent. We anticipated that we would not find the flexible structure and functions noted in our earlier sample and that the differences between the most competent, black working-class families and the most competent middle- and upper-middle-class white families would be much more apparent than the similarities.

REFERENCES

1. Parsons, T., & Bales, R. *Family, socialization and interaction process.* Glencoe, Illinois: Free Press, 1955.
2. American Psychiatric Association. *Diagnostic and statistical manual of mental disorders, Third Edition.* Washington, D.C.: American Psychiatric Association, 1980.

3. Luborsky, L. Clinician's judgments of mental health: A proposed scale. *Archives of General Psychiatry,* 1962, *7*(6), 407–417.
4. Lewis, J. M., Beavers, W. R., Gossett, J. T., & Phillips, V. A. *No single thread: Psychological health in family systems.* New York: Brunner/Mazel, 1976.
5. Gossett, J. T., Lewis, J. M., & Barnhart, F. D. *To find a way: The outcome of hospital treatment of disturbed adolescents.* New York: Brunner/Mazel, 1983.
6. Auletta, K. A reporter at large: The underclass. *The New Yorker,* November 16, 23, 30, 1981.

CHAPTER 2

The Continuum of
Family Competence

As described in the previous chapter, this study of working-class black families is based on the design and findings of our earlier study of middle- and upper-middle-class white families. The central constructs of family competence and the continuum of family competence have been articulated. In this chapter, we focus on descriptions of families at different points on the continuum of family competence.* These descriptions are based entirely on the earlier study.

The Continuum of Family Competence is presented in Figure 1. Representing the four basic levels of family competence as equal segments of the continuum is only for the convenience of illustration, for what proportion of a representative sample of families would occupy each segment is unknown. Indeed, how many families in such a sample could not be placed on the continuum (i.e., would not "fit") is also not known, although our experience suggests that such families are rare.

---

*A detailed description of the methods and data on which these descriptions are based can be found in Lewis, J. M., Beavers, W. R., Gossett, J. T., and Phillips, V. A. *No Single Thread: Psychological Health in Family Systems.* New York: Brunner/Mazel, 1976.

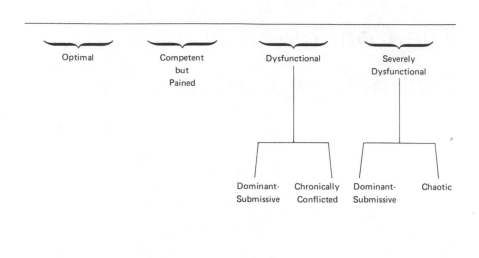

Figure 1. The Continuum of Family Competence

OPTIMAL FAMILIES

These families are rarely seen in clinical practice except under conditions of extreme external stress, such as the loss of a loved one. Those mental health professionals who have grown up in dysfunctional families, participated in the evolution of a dysfunctional current family, and now work daily with dysfunctional families and their members may doubt the existence of optimal families. In our experience, they are not rare in research volunteer samples, although whether they represent 5% or 25% of the general population remains to be determined.

It is also important to emphasize that in the following description of optimal families family "style" is not given consideration and needs, therefore, a brief notation. On the surface, optimal families differ: Some, for example, are much involved in athletic activities, and so a great deal of family life centers on sports. Such physically oriented families appear to be very different from families for whom art galleries, concert halls, and books are the center of family life. These differences in style may obscure similarities in the underlying processes of relating and communicating. However, when one shifts the level of observation from the *style* to the *pattern* of interactions that characterize the family's life together, it becomes clear that optimal families share basic aspects of family life which may be understood as the interactional structure of the family system.

Optimal families are characterized by parental marriages in which power is shared and intimacy is achieved. Leadership can be provided by either parent, depending on the context. In some optimal families leadership follows traditional gender role definitions, but this seems less important than the fact that each has areas of expertise that are acknowledged and respected by the other. The basic issue of "Who decides what?" expresses the universal need for each marital couple to come to a mutually satisfactory distribution of power within their relationship. In optimal families the process of sharing decisions seems natural and easy rather than directly discussed or deliberately planned.

In their relationships with their children, these parents are authoritative but not authoritarian. Clearly they are in charge, but family life is not dominated by multiple and rigid rules that apply under all circumstances. Rather, parents seek their children's opinions and feelings and take them into account in making decisions. For their part, the children accept this power differential without long-lasting resentment or rebellion. Beavers has used the term "growers" and "controllers" to describe two very different patterns of childrearing.[1] Optimal parents are clearly growers.

The achievement of intimacy, as we understand it, is not primarily concerned with physical sexuality, but rather with a level of communication in which two people can share deeply held feelings, thoughts, and vulnerabilities. Our assessment of a marital couple's capacity for this level of communication is based on self-report. In individual exploratory interviews, these men and women comment spontaneously on the unique openness that is characteristic of their marriages. Whether such intimacy is a daily occurrence or happens less regularly, these individuals value it highly and describe it as unique to their relationship.

The importance of physical sexuality varies greatly from couple to couple. Some couples report high frequencies of sexual intercourse (four or five times per week), while others report much lower frequen-

cies (one or two times per month). Two features of their sexual life
are prominent. Husband and wife report separately the same frequency of intercourse; that is, the husband's and wife's self-reports were
not significantly discrepant, as is often the case for couples with dysfunctional marriages. Regardless of the frequency of intercourse, both
husband and wife report high levels of sexual satisfaction.

There is no evidence of competing coalitions with others in couples
who have relationships characterized by shared power, high levels of
intimacy, and sexual satisfaction. Although children, parents, siblings,
and friends are obviously important to these men and women, there
are no other competing relationships. In particular, in our study we
found no evidence of competing parent-child coalitions that are so frequent in dysfunctional families. In a different language, there is nothing
to suggest lingering family romances or triangles.

These families are characterized by high levels of individual autonomy and yet, at the same time, by high levels of closeness. Closeness
is not purchased at the expense of individual autonomy, nor is autonomy purchased at the cost of great interpersonal distance. Autonomy
is encouraged by a family climate that facilitates each individual's
disclosing feelings and thoughts with clarity. Ambiguity is discouraged.
The family, as a group, is receptive to and, with high frequency,
acknowledges family members' communications. Each family member
takes responsibility for his or her actions, thoughts, and feelings. There
is little, if any, invasiveness in which one family member tells another
what the other is feeling or thinking. "John, you're hungry; get a cookie"
is not a typical message at this level of family competence.

These families solve problems regularly and efficiently by negotiating. Opinions are sought in the effort to reach a consensus and compro-
mises are negotiated; however, if they fail to reach a compromise, the
parents decide. It is not necessary, however, for everyone to be of one
mind.

Optimal families express a wide range of feelings, and empathic
responses to affective messages are common. Although conflicts arise,
they are dealt with, and there is no evidence of underlying, chronic,
smoldering disagreements. Generally, the family mood is warm, affectionate, humorous, and optimistic.

Members of optimal families seem to appreciate that they are fortunate in being part of such families. Their appraisals of their own

families are in agreement with those of the professionals who have rated the family videotapes. They are, however, somewhat at a loss to explain why things are going so well. The children most often ascribe it to the parents, and the parents to each other. "Anyone would be lucky to have her (him) as a wife (husband)" and "She (he) really makes it all go" are typical statements. By contrast, in many dysfunctional families what is ascribed to the other is that which is wrong, bad, sick, or evil. ("If it weren't for you" can carry either positive or negative valence.)

Other characteristics of optimal families include high levels of initiative, a tolerance for mistakes, and a veiw of human motivation as complex rather than simple. Sexuality is viewed as a natural expression. Although most of the families studied were obtained from the roster of a large Protestant church, their commitment to religion varies greatly. For some, it involves a nominal belief in God and occasional church attendance; for others religion is an important, organizing structure for family life. Members of these families respond to value surveys by ranking highly values of personal and family security, health, and happiness. Values such as world peace, the end of poverty, and equality are placed at a lower priority in forced ranking. Values are supported by rationality ("I've thought about it and that seems to be the way it adds up.") and by feelings ("I don't really know — that's just the way it feels inside."), but not by reliance on external authority ("That's the way my father, grandfather, and all my relatives have always thought.").

The husbands and wives in these families are seen as psychologically healthy, from the perspectives of both exploratory interviews and psychological tests. There are no strong neurotic traits, unusual symptoms, or use of psychoactive drugs. The men tend to be disciplined, occupationally successful, interpersonally oriented, and capable of expressing warmth directly. The women are also interpersonally oriented and active with friends and in the community; although some are employed, all derive great satisfaction from the roles of wife and mother.

The children in optimal families also are seen as psychologically healthy. They are doing well in school, have friends, and are involved in a variety of extracurricular activities. Sibling birth order appears to play a role in the children's personalities at this level of family competence. Older children, regardless of gender, are more self-disciplined, studious, and serious, whereas younger children are more open with affect, warmer, and more openly loving. These characteristics are less likely to be related to sibling birth order in dysfunctional families, where differences are gender related: Boys are more disciplined and girls more expressive regardless of sibling birth order in such families.

Descriptions of optimal families may sound as if such families are perfect. They are not, of course. Conflicts, tensions, and disagreements are part of their lives. Parents worry about their children's grades, emerging sexuality, and use of the family automobile. At times, the children feel that the parents are unfair. Everyone gets colds; adolescents have pimples; grandparents die; friends move away. Student council elections are lost. Not everyone makes the basketball team, and there is only one first chair in the violin section of the school orchestra. Disappointments and hurts, anger and fear, loss and sadness are all part of the lives of these families. Their favorable economic circumstances eliminate concerns about physical survival and so they have been able to use the freedom from such constricting concerns to good advantage in establishing a family system based on interactional patterns and structures uniquely suited for the development of parental support and adolescent autonomy. Although there are theories as to how such fortunate family systems come to be, confirmation will require longitudinal family studies, perhaps covering several generations.* It is important, however, to recognize that the parents in optimal families often describe their own families-of-origin in terms that suggest clear family dysfunction. However, despite the episodes of tension and conflict, the problems, stresses, and disappointments, these families accomplish the two cardinal tasks of the family.

COMPETENT BUT PAINED FAMILIES

Although there are no reliable epidemiologic data, clinicians who provide services to middle- and upper-middle-class patients and families would, we believe, endorse our suspicion that there are a great many families who are competent but pained. These families have both ob-

---

*The Timberlawn Psychiatric Research Foundation has currently initiated such a longitudinal study.

vious strengths and significant weaknesses. They look competent when contrasted to clearly dysfunctional families, but when they are seen against the backdrop of the optimal families, their problems are easily visible.

These families are pained, and often the mother bears the brunt of the pain. The parental marriage has not achieved a level of intimacy satisfactory to both spouses. Each, in his or her own way, ascribes the problems to the other and fails to see his or her own role. The wife feels lonely and shut out of her husband's life. "He is remote, disinterested in feelings, and keeps to himself" is her complaint. These women are often overweight, sour, and often are prescribed antianxiety agents. With but little encouragement in individual interviews, they admit that earlier dreams of the "good life" have vanished and, both angry and sad, they blame their husbands, although simultaneously acknowledging that they are good providers and caring, if isolated, fathers.

The husbands fit these descriptions. Task-oriented, compulsive, and prone to solitary pursuits, they do not value interpersonal relationships highly. Their successful careers are described in terms of instrumental goals: Relations with fellow employees are not a career-connected satisfaction. In individual interviews, most describe themselves as "loners"; they are not, however, uncomfortable with their restricted affect — at least they have not experienced such pain as they move into their 40s.

In describing their wives, these men, like their spouses, are accurate: "She's sour and has let herself go physically. She only wants to complain." They describe their wives' "nervousness" as a reflection of some physical abnormality, most often an early menopause. They acknowledge that their wives are good mothers, but find their spouses difficult to get close to or love.

The parental coalition is strained by this failure, and the consequences are clear. These couples have little private life of their own, and their time together is almost entirely child-focused. Soccer games, school activities, and recreation as a family find them together, but when not so engaged they often pursue solitary activities. Power is not handled comfortably by the sharing seen in optimal families; rather, there is either a pattern of one clearly dominant parent or a rigid division of turf with, for example, the wife making all the decisions about the children and the husband rigidly in charge of money.

There are often competing coalitions in such families and, predictably, they involve one partner who tries to replace the closeness missing in the marriage in relationships with a child, parent, or friend. It is this person with whom intimacies are exchanged and often complaints about the spouse voiced. The spouse does not complain about these relationships, but may experience them as providing greater opportunity for his or her own solitary pursuits.

This description of the problem in the competent but pained marriages fails to underscore the importance of the family to both parents. They love their children and are tremendously invested in their welfare. Whether it is the children's academic, social, athletic, or cultural aspirations, parental support and encouragement are unstinting.

In experimental family problem-solving and family interviews, factors which encourage the development of autonomy are clearly visible. Communications are clear, attentive, and respectful. Invasions or "mind-reading" are rare. However, in the affective area of family life, the parental failure in intimacy spills over. These families are much more restricted in the range of feelings expressed, demonstrate less empathy, and tend to be "polite" rather than openly affectionate. It is as if there is a heavy proscription against affective spontaneity, perhaps because such freedom with feelings would allow the underlying parental conflict to emerge.

Despite this affective constriction, competent but pained families solve problems effectively so long as the problem does not impinge directly upon the parental conflict. They see themselves as strong, but they are using clearly troubled neighbors or friends as a standard. "Although we're not perfect, we don't drink too much, fight with each other, or get a divorce—like so many do" is a typical expression of this shared attempt to see themselves in a favorable light.

The children flourish, however; in school, social activities, and extracurricular pursuits, they do well. They are rated as "healthy" in both exploratory interviews and psychological tests. As a group they are indistinguishable from the children of optimal families. This finding lends itself to two interpretations: one, that children do not need an optimal environment in order to achieve psychological health—given a halfway decent opportunity they will do well; or two, that longitudinal studies are necessary— more of these children than those from optimal families may well have trouble down the road. In particular, some would caution, one would look for differences after the children have become adults and married. The pessimists anticipate that more from this group will have troubled marriages — that, for some, there will be an intergenerational transmission of both marital object choices and patterns of marital interaction. The truth, of course, is that we do not know. All that can be said is that as adolescents they look like the well functioning children from optimal families.

Competent but pained families are characterized by the failure of the parents to achieve a mutually satisfactory level of intimacy. The other aspects of family life that are less than what is achieved by optimal families can be related to this flaw. This speaks to the importance of the parental marriages as the foundation of the family. Indeed, independent ratings of the parent's relationship (without the children) and the total family competence ratings were positively correlated at statistically significant levels. It is difficult for a family to function optimally if the parental marriage is clearly troubled.

DYSFUNCTIONAL FAMILIES

Dysfunctional families flounder to a significant degree in accomplishing both of the cardinal tasks of the family. For the most part, clinicians treat primarily dysfunctional or severely dysfunctional families. In our middle- and upper-middle-class clinical setting, dysfunctional families are the rule, while the severely dysfunctional families are the exception. This may not, however, represent the actual distribution of these two groups of families in this socioeconomic population; rather, it may be related more clearly to help-seeking patterns. The absence of careful epidemiologic studies underlies this uncertainty.

Dysfunctional families can be described either macroscopically or microscopically. Our approach is first to ascertain fairly gross patterns, and then to move to microscopic observations. At the macroscopic level, two distinct patterns of dysfunctional families can be seen: the dominant-submissive and the chronically conflicted.

The dominant-submissive family is characterized by the presence of one strongly dominant parent who controls (or attempts to control) every aspect of family life. This dominant parent can be either the mother or the father, but in our experience is most often the latter. The submissive spouse's role within the family is much more like that of a child. He or she is dependent, passive, or peripheral to most of what is going on in the family. An important consideration involves the degree to which this marital pattern of dominance and submission is complementary, that is, acceptable and satisfying for both participants. Although such families are seen in both clinical and research volunteer samples, it is perhaps more common in clinical practice to see families in which there is open conflict over the unequal power in the marital relationship.

The submissive spouse is apt to resent the position of powerlessness, regardless of how much he or she invites the spouse's domination. This often leads to a coalition involving the submissive spouse and one of the children, who presents as the "identified" patient. The submissive spouse may obtain vicarious gratification from the child's symptomatic behavior because the dominant spouse is unable to control the child's behavior.

The dominant spouse may come to feel overwhelmed, burdened, or clinically depressed, both because the responsibility that goes with controlling everything comes to be stressful and because the position of dominance keeps others at a distance and leads eventually to loneliness.

Dominant-submissive families become permeated by the controllingness of the dominant spouse, and there is little closeness. There is often a baseline mood of either hostility or depression in such families. Expression of feelings is markedly restricted, empathy rare, and the chronic family conflict omnipresent. These families do not negotiate, and their problem-solving usually reflects only the dominant parent's thoughts. There is much blaming in these families and little encouragement to accept responsibility for one's own actions because doing so may well invoke the wrath and heightened controllingness of the dominant parent.

Children growing up in these families are at risk for significant psychopathology. Often one child is scapegoated, and it is clear that his or her behavior diverts attention from the parental conflict. Behavioral disturbances are seen in such children, but the psychopathology may take other forms, such as severe neuroses or reactive psychotic episodes. In research volunteer families, one sometimes sees dominant-submissive families without a clearly identifiable patient. Despite the level of family disturbance and discomfort, the children often have difficulty in separating from the family. One may speculate that growing up in a context in which one's own inclinations are constantly subjugated by the control of another may make facing the uncertainties and developmental challenges of young adulthood more difficult.

The chronically conflicted type of dysfunctional family is a second distinct pattern seen in clinical samples, although it is rarely seen in research volunteer cohorts. This type of dysfunctional family is easily identifiable by the presence of chronic, unresolvable parental conflict. The parents appear to be at war and, although the substance of their interminable battles may change, there is always conflict. It is as if the parents have not resolved the basic issue of power in their relationship, and each new family decision reopens this conflict. While the parents in optimal families share power comfortably and dominant-submissive families reveal a skewed or clearly unequal distribution of power, parents in chronically conflicted families contend endlessly for power. Each spouse tries to dominate and neither will accept the submissive role; thus, they avoid underlying fears of closeness or intimacy (whether consciously or unconsciously).

The pattern of parental conflict is remarkably similar from one battle to another and usually escalates rapidly. The initial conflict-producing decision is quickly left behind as the parental accusations become increasingly personal—often culminating with attacks on each other's masculinity, femininity, or basic worth as a person. Manipulative behavior is common; the children are used as pawns, first on one side, then the other. The family climate is dominated by accusations, blaming, manipulations, exploitation, and great distance between family members. It is an environment in which trust is absent and self-centeredness prevails.

Conflicted families are inefficient in problem-solving because the presentation of a problem evokes yet another round of the parental battle. Such families are disagreeable to be a part of, and the children may respond by running away or attempting to establish membership in other groups. Chronically conflicted families are seldom found in research volunteer samples; presumably either they cannot agree to participate or their level of distrust is too intense. They often are seen, however, in clinical samples. Usually a child is the identified patient.

SEVERELY DYSFUNCTIONAL FAMILIES

These families fail profoundly in accomplishing the two cardinal tasks of the family. There are often several family members with clearly manifest, severe, chronic psychopathology.

There are two subtypes of severely dysfunctional families: the dominant-submissive and the chaotic. The dominant-submissive family is organized around and dominated by one parent, who is often paranoid or otherwise psychotic. His or her perception and cognition are the accepted reality of the family. The other spouse is ineffective and unable to buffer the destructive impact of the disturbed and dominant parent. The children grow up in an environment that blurs self-boundaries, distorts reality, and fosters persistent symbiotic attachments.

The chaotic, severely dysfunctional family has neither a leader nor a dominant, albeit psychotic, person around which the family is organized. Rather, no one has sufficient ego strength and interpersonal influence to provide a stable structure for the family. As a consequence, the family drifts aimlessly, with its members often accepting a fused existence with no movement toward individuation and autonomy. At the same time, such families are relatively impervious to the surrounding world. They have few ongoing relationships with others, except, perhaps, the parents' families of origin. Here the parents relate most often as little children who continue their pattern of extreme dependency.

Denial and projection are the mainstays of both types of severely dysfunctional families. "We are a very healthy family" can be articulated by such families even when several of the members are grossly psychotic, the family totally unable to solve problems, and the mood of the family one of hopelessness. Little is done to encourage individual autonomy; communication is unclear, permeability of low order, and invasions of each others' minds common.

In these families severe parental communication deviance provides a training ground for the development of thought disturbances in vulnerable children. Such families do not often seek professional help on their own; rather, they come to the clinic because of the intervention of an external community authority. If the clinical situation involves one of the children, that child is most often seen as having either a severe borderline disturbance or a schizophrenic syndrome of chronic duration and with many process features. Frequently, however, several members of the family have severe and chronic psychiatric syndromes.

FLEXIBILITY, RIGIDITY, AND CHAOS

These brief descriptions of families at various levels of family competence are intended to communicate something of the nature of the strengths and liabilities of a wide range of families. Although there are differences within groups of families at any level of family competence, the structural patterns are usually clear. What may need repeated emphasis is that at the optimal end of the continuum are families with clear structure and flexibility. An observer has no difficulty ascertaining the interactional patterns that comprise the family structure. At the same time, these are families with a wide range of responses to changing circumstances. They react quickly and efficiently to changes or stress. If their initial response is not effective, they move to another. They have well developed feedback mechanisms and creative response patterns.

This is in striking contrast to dysfunctional families. Both dominant-submissive and chronically conflicted families have limited response repertoires and adhere rigidly to them. Dominant-submissive families respond to stress or change by increasing the level of internal controls. On the surface this appears to reflect the dominant parent's response, but the submissive spouse and children participate subtly. It is, in short, a total system response. The chronically conflicted family, on the other hand, responds to stress or change by increasing the conflict. Neither of these subtypes of families considers options, changes directions, or experiments with novel approaches. Whether it is the increased internal control of the dominant-submissive family or the increased level of conflict of the chronically-conflicted family, it is the stereotyped response that characterizes such family systems.

At the severely dysfunctional end of the Continuum of Family Competence, the dominant-submissive subtype is a rigidly controlled system with frequent breakdown of the psychotic, dominant parent's control, resulting in disorganization and periods of chaos. The chaotic subtype

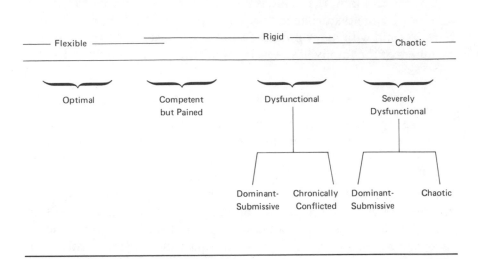

Figure 2. Underlying Structure of Families on the Continuum of Family Competence.

is consistently disorganized in an aimless, drifting state. Both of these types of families are grossly deficient in solving problems, and they survive as social systems by virtue of shared primitive mechanisms that result in significant distortion of the world around them.

It can be seen that the fundamental structural configurations of families at various points on the Continuum of Family Competence range from clear structure with flexible operations (optimal families) to clear structure with rigid operations (dysfunctional families) to unclear structures and disorganized operations (severely dysfunctional families). This pattern of flexibility→rigidity→chaos is illustrated in Figure 2.

STRESS AND THE STRUCTURE OF THE FAMILY

It is important to emphasize that families are not fixated at one point on the Continuum of Family Competence but, under certain circumstances, may move from one position to another. Longitudinal family studies are needed to document whether the developmental challenges involved in traversing the family life cycle result in major structural alteration in the family. Our studies to date are restricted to families in one stage of development, that is, families with adolescent children. Whether families at different stages of the life cycle would demonstrate the same range of structural configurations is not known. Skynner, for example, has emphasized that structural alterations in families occur as part of family development.[2] His theoretical scheme, derived from clinical work, involves the central role of more primitive, dependent relationships early in the family life cycle. He suggests that when children are beyond infancy the structural configuration of the family changes and issues of firmness, control, and authority are paramount. Only somewhat later in the life cycle does Skynner anticipate the kind of sharing we found in families containing adolescents. He emphasizes also that the concepts of fixation and regression have relevance for family functioning. A family with children in late adolescence that is still centrally concerned with rigid controls would be seen either as fixated at the earlier stage of family development or as having regressed to it because of underlying shared anxiety or conflict emanating from the developmental challenges of that phase of the family life cycle. Skynner's work shows a striking parallel to our own and may be seen as supporting the validity of the structural aspects of the Continuum of Family Competence.

The response of the family system to stress also sheds light on the validity of the Continuum of Family Competence. Stress may originate either within the family system or external to and impinging upon it. In the first instance, we refer both to stress that emanates from internal patterns of interaction that lead to conflict (as in dysfunctional families) and to stress that results when patterns of family interaction interfere with or impede the development of individuation and autonomy in family members (as in severely dysfunctional families). From this perspective it is possible to understand the Continuum of Family Competence as a reflection of the amount and impact of internal family stress on the structural configuration of the family.

Anthony's studies of the impact of external stress on the family provide another source of validation of the Continuum of Family Competence.[3] He examined the changes occurring in families when facing the possible death of a family member. These studies demonstrate that some families with clear structure and flexible operations may respond to such stress by changes in structure, moving, in particular, towards a structural realignment in which one family member assumes increasing authority and control. This family member may reach a position of considerable dominance and, in this way, families seen as optimal may have changed to more clearly approximate our description of dominant-submissive dysfunctional families. Under these circumstances there is a diminution in affective freedom, capacity for negotiation, and other characteristics typical of their prior, optimal level of functioning.

Anthony indicates that under conditions of prolonged stress, the family structural configuration may undergo further change, and he describes a movement towards increasing disorganization. If the stress continues and if interventions by others are absent or ineffective, family members appear to become disconnected and there develops an aimless, drifting quality to the family. In effect, Anthony has described families moving from flexibility to rigidity to chaos.

These changes may also occur in the opposite direction. Family therapists have noted that chaotic families may, as a result of intensive interventions, move towards clearer, albeit rigid, structural realignments. Rigid families may change in the direction of greater flexibility, more openness, increased affective expressiveness, greater empathy, and more shared power.

Changes in family structure can be seen both as responsive to internal or external stress and as adaptive in the sense that they represent the attempt to contain or bind the stress in order to prevent disorganization and the ultimate disintegration of the family system. Family therapists have emphasized that the development of psychiatric symptoms in a family member may represent, at least in part, an attempt to focus and contain family stress and stabilize the family (even at a dysfunctional level) to avoid disorganization and disintegration. Exactly how this occurs is not clear, but some feel that it is by redirecting the attention of the family away from the serious family system problem and onto one family member.

Much remains to be learned about the factors that facilitate or impede transformations of family structure either as part of the family life cycle or in response to stress. Our research findings, as well as the work of other investigators and clinicians, support the validity of the

Continuum of Family Competence. Most studies, however, are based on intact, middle-class families with adolescent children. The direct impact of factors such as socioeconomic status and ethnicity remains to be explored from this perspective.

REFERENCES

1. Beavers, W. R. *Psychotherapy and growth: A family systems perspective.* New York: Brunner/Mazel, 1977.
2. Skynner, A. C. R. *Systems of marital and family psychotherapy.* New York: Brunner/Mazel, 1976.
3. Anthony, J. E. The impact of mental and physical illness on family life. *American Journal of Psychiatry,* 1970, *127,* 138–146.

CHAPTER 3

Method and Sample

Although both the measures for studying lower-income, intact families and the factors leading to a focus on working-class families are decribed in Chapter 1, it is important to spell out in detail the criteria used in the final selection of the sample. There are a number of factors that need emphasis in order to delineate the ways in which this sample differs from the previously studied middle- and upper-middle-class white families. These are socioeconomic status, the definition of intactness, the stage of family development, and the definition of family competence.

The difficulties encountered in locating intact families with incomes below the poverty level have been noted. As these became apparent and the realities of the project's limited funding became increasingly apparent, a decision was made to use as a target a total family income (before taxes) of $10,000 or lower, but even this compromise resulted in a wider range of family incomes than anticipated. The major reason for this was the discrepancy between the incomes determined for some families at the time of their acceptance into the project and that understood at the time data collection was completed. Despite questioning, a number of the families initially underreported their total incomes. As a research alliance developed, however, the research team learned of a part-time second job of a father, some income-producing childcare of a mother, and the contributions made through jobs of the children.

A second issue involved the definition of intactness. Although this was not a problem in our earlier study of more affluent families, it proved to be with this sample. In some of the families there was a younger child who was not the biological child of the parents, but was the child of one of their young adult children. These families were direct and open about this fact and dealt with it as a natural circumstance. Another complication in several of the families was that the father was not the biologic parent of some of the children. Often this involved a child who was the product of an earlier adolescent or young adult relationship of the mother. There was no defensiveness about this circumstance, and it is clear that within this sample there is a fluid and flexible definition of the family.

A third issue concerns the stage of family development. In our earlier work the families were selected with the oldest child in middle or late adolescence, and the only exceptions involved a 19- or 20-year old sibling who was away at college or in military service. Many of the families in this sample had older children not living at home in addition to their adolescents.

A final factor involved the operational definition of a competent family. In our earlier work we used as an initial screening device the criteria that no member of the family had received any form of mental health care or been involved in any legal difficulty during the preceding two years. This screening device had produced a group of families ranging from those rated as highly competent to those that were clearly dysfunctional. (Severely dysfunctional families, in our experience, did not volunteer for family studies.) The same criteria were stated in this project. It is important, however, to point out that this study, like the earlier one, was described to potential participants and various community resources as a study of family health. Actually, the use of words such as "healthy," "competent," and "adaptive" were often met with quizzical looks. A pastor who identified several families for us stated, "I don't know exactly how to make sense of what you mean when you use words like that to describe what you are looking for, but I do have some *strong* families in my congregation." When asked what he meant by "strong" he said, "They stay together, Mom and Dad get along, when one is down the other one helps. They believe in their children and their children grow up to be good citizens."

This pastor's definition of "strong" contains the elements described by Parsons as primary functions of the family, that is, stabilizing parental personalities and developing autonomous children.[1] As described in Chapter 1, it corresponds closely to our value judgments of what families with adolescent children "ought" to do, upon which the Continuum of Family Competence is based. The operational definition of family competence used in this study is identical to that used in the earlier study, namely, the two factors emphasized by Parsons and articulated by the pastor. The difference lies in our major hypothesis. We predicted that the most competent families in this sample would demonstrate a significant structural difference from that found in the more affluent families and that the difference would be in the direction of increased rigidity.

THE COMPOSITION OF THE RESEARCH TEAM

In the research team's preliminary discussions, the decision was made to add one or more black professionals to the team. There was general agreement that it was necessary for black colleagues to be involved in the collection, evaluation, and analysis of the research data. This procedure was followed, and we believe worked well, but in retrospect it may be that we were struggling with what Merton has called the insider-outsider dilemma (the researcher must be black, white, Catholic, or Jewish in order to understand black, white, Catholic, or Jewish persons, families, or social structures).[2] At the time this decision was made, all members of the team were white and all of our prior research experience had been with white families; it seems probable that, at some level, we were dealing with some uncertainty about whether black colleagues would have special insights into black social-psychological phenomena.

Three persons comprised the data collection team. Carolyn Meador is a black registered nurse enrolled in graduate school who hoped to use her role in this project as a basis for her graduate dissertation. She was responsible for contacting potential research families, early negotiating of a research alliance, and collecting significant amounts of the data. She did the structured, demographic interviews and was responsible for videotaping the family interactional testing. She was a full-time member of the team.

John G. Looney is a white child psychiatrist with prior research experience. He was employed one-quarter time and had broad responsibilities as the co-principal investigator. These responsibilities included participating in planning the study, establishing the community alliances that led to identifying potential research families, conducting individual and family interviews, and writing substantial sections of this book.

Truman Thomas, M.S., was a part-time member of the research team who was primarily involved in data collection. A black male social worker, this colleague was employed in an agency serving the area in which many of the families lived. He was involved in contacting families, conducting individual interviews, and rating interview transcripts.

The senior author, Jerry M. Lewis, co-principal investigator, is a psychiatrist, clinician, and researcher. He supervised the design of the study and the data analysis and was responsible for this manuscript reporting the findings.

Other members of the research team (John T. Gossett, Ph.D., F. David Barnhart, M.A., Virginia Austin Phillips, and Charles B. Thomas, Ph.D.) were involved in rating individual interviews, scoring paper-and-pencil tests, rating family videotapes, data analysis, and helping prepare the manuscript. All were part-time and represented the disciplines of sociology, social psychology, and clinical psychology. All are white except Charles Thomas, a black social psychologist.

In summary, both black and white professionals were involved in all phases of this project. No consistent differences across ethnic lines were found in the evaluation of the data. All members of the research team were, however, members of the broad middle-class.

LOCATING THE SAMPLE

Although difficulties were anticipated, the research team underestimated the effort required to locate and obtain the cooperation of the sample. In particular, establishing an alliance with leaders in the black community who would support the research effort and help locate families was more complex than originally anticipated.

The initial effort focused on the staff of a neighborhood health clinic, which provided adolescents with a broad range of health care, including the treatment of physical illness, birth control counseling, and psychological counseling for a variety of problems of living. Several members of the research team were friends of the physicians at the clinic. The research team met with the entire clinical staff and described the project. The reaction was mixed — some staff members were enthusiastic and others wary. In subsequent meetings, clinic staff members articulated a protective attitude towards their patients, which came from a concern that many previous studies of poor, black families in their neighborhood had been used to describe life in such families negatively and, most importantly, had been used as a basis for reduction in services funded by the government.

The clinic staff referred the research team to a group of influential neighborhood pastors, indicating that they could "make or break" the study. In addition, the clinic staff referred the research team to other influential individuals whose support might be helpful.

Involvement with the pastors' group (an informal ministerial alliance) proved to be crucial. A series of steps was necessary, however, before they identifed potential families. The first hurdle involved lengthy meetings in which the goals of the project were examined and dissected. Following these discussions, the value orientations of the two researchers were examined, particularly as they might interface with religious values. Throughout this phase of the discussions, considerable distrust of psychiatry and psychology was voiced — most often around the issue of Godlessness.

When the discussions were concluded, the researchers received invitations to Saturday morning and evening meetings of the pastors' group. At these meetings a meal would be prepared and served, followed by a religious service preparing the pastor for the next day's church services. One researcher (J.G.L.) was invited to preach about the research project at several such services. Then a Saturday meal and meeting were held at the Timberlawn Research Foundation. By the end of several months of these exchanges, most of the pastors favored supporting the research project; at this point, they referred what appeared to be a "pilot" family — one of their own group — a family in which the father was an associate pastor. The feedback from this family was positive, and more family referrals followed.

This time-consuming process resulted in the development of a strong alliance with the pastors' group and, ultimately, the referral of six families. The other families came from two additional sources. About one-third were referred by families who were studied early in the project. The remaining families came from the student government at a large, predominantly black public high school, whose principal understood the project and knew and trusted two members of the research team (J.M.L. and J.G.L.). The study was "adopted" by the student government, and its members became active in locating families.

The three sources of families identified about 80 families as potential participants. Of these, however, 60 families failed to meet the criteria for the study, primarily because their total family income exceeded $10,000.

INSTRUMENTS AND DATA COLLECTION

The instruments used in this project were designed to collect data at different levels: that of the individual family member and that of the family as a group. In selecting specific instruments to be used, the research team sought to replicate the earlier study as closely as possible, except when subsequent research publications suggested a more appropriate instrument or when other instruments had been developed in the interval since the earlier study.

Applying instruments developed with one socioeconomic or ethnic group to other populations raises many complex questions. We made every effort to ascertain whether or not working-class black families had been part of the population from which the instruments had been derived. Often, however, information about this was unclear or inconclusive. In instances when such instruments are used, it is very important to emphasize the multiple and equally valid interpretations of results that are possible.

The instruments designed to obtain data from individual family members were structured and semi-structured interviews and a variety of paper-and-pencil tests.*

---

*See Appendix B for instruments.

Demographic Interview

This structured interview with each family member elicits information about the individual's current life. The interviewer tried, in addition, to conduct the interview in a way that would further the developing research alliance. This instrument was developed at the Foundation and used in the earlier study.

Exploration of Current Functioning

This semi-structured interview investigates the individual's perceptions of himself or herself in the family, work or school, social networks, and avocational pursuits. In addition, the instrument elicits predominant feelings about the individual's niche in the world. This instrument was developed by the research team and used in the earlier study.

Three-generation Survey

The primary focus of this semi-structured interview was the parents' families of origin. The interview is designed to obtain a comprehensive picture of the circumstances of each parent's childhood and his or her feelings about those circumstances. The interview also probed current relationships with these grandparents and other relatives. This instrument was developed at the Foundation and was used in the earlier study.

Medical History

A structured interview was used for gathering the medical history of each family member. This included current physical health status, past serious illnesses, chronic diseases, surgical procedures, and utilization of health care services. The same interview was used in the earlier study.

Family Characteristics Inventory

This is a 50-item self-administered questionnaire assessing each individual's perception of family life. Each of the items is scored on a five-point scale ranging from "Does not fit our family at all" to "Fits our family very well." The inventory was developed at the Foundation for use in earlier studies. Each family member completes the inventory independently, which allows appraisal of the amount of agreement within a family as well as the comparison of family means for each item.

Family Closeness Board

This is a hardwood board with holes drilled in it in the shape of a spiral. Each individual is asked to place peg dolls representing family members into the holes in a way that reflects the individual's perception of the closeness of each family member to other family members. The spiral arrangement of the holes precludes the use of equal distances between dolls. Individuals complete the task independently. This instrument was developed at the Foundation in order to facilitate a family discussion on closeness in the family, which was one portion of a standard family interaction format.

The California Psychological Inventory

This is a 480-item personality measure that is widely used. It is considered to discriminate levels of function among normal populations and was used in this study rather than the Minnesota Multiphasic Personality Inventory used in the earlier study.

The Shipley-Hartford Vocabulary Scale and Abstraction Scale

This test is a short and simple alternative to the more comprehensive intelligence measures with which it correlates. It was used in the early study of more affluent white families.

The Rokeach Value Survey

This is a widely used survey of an individual's value preferences. Its format is a forced ranking procedure of two lists of 18 terminal and instrumental values. This survey was used in the previous study.

The Offer Adolescent Self-image Questionnaire

This is a 130-item, self-administered instrument in which each adolescent rates various aspects of his or her self-image on 12-point scales. This measure was not available at the time of our earlier study.

Exploratory Psychiatric Interview

This is a partially structured interview in which the interviewer, an experienced clinician, investigates the individual's ability to work, love, and play. The capacity for work was judged by the individual's self-report regarding performance and pleasure at the job, in the home, or at school. The capacity for love was approached by exploring the individual's relationships within the family and social network, with a particular focus on the report of psychological intimacy within relationships. Play was assessed by exploring the individual's participation in leisure activities. These interviews were tape-recorded and transcribed. The transcripts were de-identified and randomly ordered and rated by three members of the research team on a five-point, overall social competence scale.

The measures used to evaluate the functioning of the family as a system included family interactional testing and an exploratory family interview. In contrast to our earlier study, with these families the family interactional testing was accomplished in their homes rather than at the Foundation.

Family Interaction Testing

This procedure is described in detail in a previous publication.[3] The family is presented with five problems to solve. The instructions for each problem are audiotaped, and the family has 10 minutes in which to solve each problem. The entire 50-minute testing is videotaped with only the family members in the room.

The first task involves the entire family in discussing "Family Strengths." The second task begins with an audiotaped family vignette in which a family member is seriously ill, comatose, and hospitalized. The family asks the doctor whether the sick family member is going to die, and the doctor's response is ambiguous. At this point the vignette stops and the family is asked to complete the story. This task challenges the family to deal with the subject of death and dying.

The third task is directed to the parents without the presence of the children. They are asked to discuss the "best" and "worst" aspects of their marriage. The fourth task, "Discuss Closeness in your Family," invites the family to talk about their relationship with each other. The use of the Family Closeness Board by each family member immediately prior to this family discussion is an attempt to facilitate thinking and talking about this subject. The final task is "Plan Something Together," in which the family is asked to plan a family activity. This task is the least charged emotionally.

Each family's 50-minute videotape was scored by three raters who were blind to other data about the family. The Beavers-Timberlawn Family Rating Scales were used. The raters' scoring of each family's global health-pathology (a measure of overall family competence) was the basis for ranking the families on the Continuum of Family Competence.

Family Interview

This interview with the family as a group explores the family's response in five areas: money, religion, education, support systems and expectations for the future (in five and ten years). The interviewer (J.G.L. or T.T.) introduces each topic in the form of an open-ended question and then attempts to facilitate the family's discussion. Only after the family appears to exhaust the subject does he play a more active, questioning role. The interviews were videotaped in the home.

In addition to the insights gained from viewing family interactional processes and from the content of the family's discussion, the research team developed a series of Family Value Transmission Scales. However, the outside raters, although achieving satisfactory interrater reliability in their training phase, did not do so in scoring the interview videotapes. As a consequence, we have no data to present regarding the transmission of family values and exploration of this important area must await further development of the scales.

THE PROCESS OF THE RESEARCH

In the study of more affluent families, data were collected at the Foundation, in the families' homes, and on job locations. The families had automobiles and were able and willing to come to the Foundation for part of the data collection. All of the family interactional testing and family interviews and some of the individual measures were accomplished at the Foundation. In the present study, however, this was not possible. Family members did not have time during the day for research procedures, and often they did not have transportation. As a consequence, all of the data were collected at the home and many visits were necessary.

During the time when contacts were being established with the individual and agency resources in the neighborhood, one of the principal investigators (J.G.L.) spent several days exploring the neighborhood in his car and on foot, developing a firsthand overview of the social context and geography.

Each family was contacted by telephone or personal visit in order to acquaint the family with the nature of the project, establish the family's ability to qualify for the study, and begin the process of building a research alliance. Later, two researchers (J.G.L. and C.M.) visited the family together, and an initial informed consent form was signed.

The next stage of the research involved home visits in order to complete the individual measures. Some of these instruments are lengthy, and the process was time-consuming for subjects with poor reading skills, because a research team member had to read each item to the subject.

The third phase of data collection involved the family interactional testing and the family interview. Following these procedures, each family signed a second consent form indicating that, having completed their involvement with the project, they allowed us to use their data, de-identified to protect their anonymity.

All of the families appeared to have derived much satisfaction from their participation. Although the intensity of the research alliance varied, most of the families were very positive in both their statements and their behavior towards the process of the research and the members of the research team.

THE SAMPLE

The number of families in this sample was cut from 20 to 18 following the collection of data. One family was dropped when it became apparent that the total family income for the reporting year represented an exception to their socioeconomic status over time. Although low enough to meet the criteria in that year, the family's income over the years had been substantially greater. A second family was dropped when it became apparent that the "parents" were actually the grandparents of a large number of cousins living together as siblings. This group appeared to fall outside even the project's liberal definition of "family."

A sample of 18 families can be considered large or small, depending on the nature of the research hypotheses being tested. We consider it a moderate size sample if consideration is given both to the hypotheses being tested and the intensity with which each family was studied. It is, however, in the further subdivision of the sample, as, for example, in contrasting the most and least competent families, that interpretations must be made with great caution. In our earlier research we studied a pilot group of 11 families and a replication group of 33 families. This sample of 18 families might well be considered a comparable pilot group, and the question can be raised regarding why we did not move ahead and study a larger replication group. There are two answers to that question. The first involves our judgment that our findings are important to many in the mental health disciplines, and the second involves the difficulty in these times of finding funding for psychosocial research in psychiatry. In the final analysis, the reader must judge about our sample size for himself or herself.

The fathers' ages were from 45 to 68 years, with a mean of 50 years. The mothers' ages were from 34 to 58, with a mean of 45 years. The average duration of the parental marriage was 24 years. Six of the fathers and seven of the mothers had earlier marriages during adolescence or young adulthood. The 18 families contained from one to ten children, with a mean of 5.3 children. However, only from one to six of the families' children remained in the home (mean of 3.2 children).

Two of the fathers were unemployed and two were retired. The remainder worked full-time: three as receiving clerks, three in construction, and two doing yard work. The others were employed in a variety of semi-skilled jobs. The average length of employment in the current job was 10 years. Six of the 18 fathers also had part-time "moonlighting" jobs.

Nine of the mothers were not wage earners, and five were employed as domestics or baby-sitters. The other four were employed as a press operator, a housekeeper, a telephone operator, and a caseworker. Those working outside the home had been employed in their current jobs for an average of six years.

The total family incomes were from $6,600 to $15,320, with a mean of $11,080. This compares with the 1978 national median for all two-parent, black families of $15,913. The comparable figure for black families in which both parents are employed outside the home is $22,125.[4]

Another method of assessing these families' socioeconomic statuses is the use of the Hollingshead Four Factor Index of Social Status.*[5] Using this index, two of the families are assigned a social class estimate of "3" (skilled craftsmen, clerical, and sales), 11 of the families are assigned an estimate of "4" (semi-skilled), and five of the families are assigned an estimate of "5" (unskilled labor and menial).

A third way of assessing the families' socioeconomic status involves comparing each family's total income to the size-adjusted family poverty level.[6] Doing so for these 18 families reveals that total incomes of 15 families are above the size-adjusted poverty levels (from $686 to $8,216 above) and incomes of three families are below them ($775, $5,280, and $5,680 below). The median for the entire group of 18 families is $3,720 above the size-adjusted poverty levels.

---

*The four factors are education, occupation, gender, and marital status.

Another approach to developing an overview of these families' social reality concerns their housing. The families live in neighborhoods which vary from lower middle-class to very low income and are populated almost entirely by blacks. In each neighborhood, however, there is great variation from street to street and even from house to house. Often, a well-kept house is next to a shack. Fifteen of the families live in houses they are purchasing, two live in rental houses, and one lives in a housing project apartment.

There was wide variation in the upkeep of the outside of the homes. Some were well-maintained, with neat yards and shrubs, while others were unpainted, with broken windows and yards filled with junk. There was similar variation in the interiors of these homes. Although the furnishings were, at best, modest, some of the interiors were neat, orderly, and clean, while others were dirty and chaotic. There was a relationship between total family income and the appearance of the housing (means of $11,777 for "better" appearing homes and $9,685 for "worse" appearing), but a few families with higher incomes lived in unpainted shacks with junk-littered yards, and several families with lower incomes had well-maintained homes and yards.

The fathers achieved an average of nine years of education (range two to 13 years), and the mothers ten years (range three to 12 years). One-half of the parents had grown up in rural settings. Six of the fathers and five of the mothers described their childhoods as both economically and emotionally deprived. As a group the fathers came from large families (mean of 7 siblings) and their parents had an average of a sixth grade education. Three of the fathers grew up without the presence of a father, and two others lost their mothers during early childhood. All but one of the fathers perceived their families-of-origin to be authoritarian, with ten describing father "in charge," five describing mother as the "boss," and two describing a grandparent as running the family. Only two of the fathers felt close to their fathers, whereas ten felt very close to their mothers.

As a group the mothers also came from large families (mean of 6.3 siblings). Thirteen of the mothers grew up with fathers in the house and reported the fathers' educational attainment as an average of five years. All their mothers were present during their childhoods, and these mothers had attained an average of eight years of education. Fifteen of these women described authoritarian families-of-origin, with nine seeing mother and six seeing father as the dominant parent. The mothers were equally divided, however, insofar as feeling closer to mother or father.

Seven of the fathers and nine of the mothers were actively involved in their churches. Nine of the fathers and 11 of the mothers were active in child-related organizations (PTA, Scouting, etc.).

Four of the 36 parents had serious or life-threatening medical conditions, and 12 of the parents felt they had some degree of disability from chronic disease. Of the latter, 11 had hypertension and five had clinically significant arthritis.

In summary, most of the parents came from large, relatively uneducated families which they perceived as authoritarian in structure. A sizeable minority recalled considerable economic and emotional deprivation. They had relatively large families and half the wives were employed. Their total family incomes varied considerably, with most several thousand dollars above the poverty level.

REFERENCES

1. Parsons, T., & Bales, R. *Family, socialization and interaction process.* Glencoe, Illinois: Free Press, 1955.
2. Merton, R. K. Insiders and outsiders: A chapter in the sociology of knowledge. *American Journal of Sociology,* July, 1972, *78,* 9–48.
3. Lewis, J. M., Beavers, W. R., Gossett, J. T., & Phillips, V. A. *No single thread: Psychological health in family systems.* New York: Brunner/Mazel, 1976.
4. U.S. Bureau of the Census, reported in the *Dallas Morning News,* August 21, 1981.
5. Hollingshead, A. B. *Four factor index of social status.* Working paper. P.O. Box 1965 Yale Station, New Haven, Connecticut 06520, 1975.
6. U.S. Department of Labor, reported in the *Dallas Morning News,* March 26, 1981.

CHAPTER 4

Findings

The findings are presented as they relate to hypotheses examined in this project:

1) Within this sample of intact, working-class black families, there will be considerable diversity in structure and function. This hypothesis leads to three research questions:
   a. What is the degree of variability in family structure and function within this sample?
   b. What are the differences between the *families* rated at the extremes of family competence?
   c. What are the differences between *individuals* comprising the families rated at the extremes of family competence?
2) The working-class families rated as most competent will demonstrate differences from the most competent middle- and upper-middle-class white families studied earlier. In the working-class sample we predicted a moderately rigid, dominant-submissive family structure with the wife-mother more often the dominant parent. This family structure will be in contrast to the pattern of shared power and joint parental leadership demonstrated in the most competent middle- and upper-middle-class families. This hypothesis is tested with the following question:
   What are the similarities and differences between the most competent families in this sample of working-class families and the most competent families in the more affluent sample?

The data that relate to these questions are presented in this chapter and Chapters 5 and 6.

THE VARIABILITY OF FAMILY STRUCTURE AND FUNCTION

There are profound differences between families in this group. Although they share many demographic features and are imbedded in the same broad sociocultural context, structure and function range from families rated as optimal to those rated as significantly dysfunctional.

Three raters (J.M.L., J.T.G., C.T.), blind to other data, based their ratings on the 50 minutes of videotaped family testing. On the 10-point Global Health-Pathology Scale, a measure of overall family competence, the raters demonstrated significant agreement (Pearsonian Correlation Coefficients $.56 - .65$, $p < .01$).

The ratings for the families ranged from families who received mostly 1's, 2's, or 3's to those families receiving mostly 7's and 8's. The range can be noted in Figure 3.

The importance of this finding is the demonstration of the broad range of family competence in a nonclinical sample of families. The absence of families rated as severely dysfunctional in a population of research volunteer families is not surprising. Although severely dysfunctional families are seen in clinical samples, they are often both suspicious and chaotic and so decline or are unable to participate in research activities.

Another approach to illustrating the range of family competence in

Figure 3. Distribution of Families on Scale of Global Health-Pathology*

							x			
			x				x			
	x	x		x			x			
	x	x	x	x	x	x	x	x	x	x
1	2	3	4		5	6	7	8	9	10
Optimal			Competent			Dysfunctional		Severely Dysfunctional		

*Average of three raters

this sample of families is the ratings on the 13 subscales of the Beavers-Timberlawn Family Evaluation Scales.* The three raters agreed at significant levels ($p < .05$) on 26 of the 39 comparisons. The Pearson Correlation Coefficients for each rater's sum of the subscales ranged from .57 to .68 ($p < .01$). The range of subscale ratings can be illustrated by comparing the mean scores for the five families rated as most competent with those for the five families rated as least competent (Table 1).

As can be noted in Table 1, 12 of the 13 comparisons of mean subscale scores for the most and least competent families are significantly different, and all are in the expected direction. This is not surprising since, theoretically, each rater uses his or her subscale ratings to arrive at a global health-pathology score. The mean scores point to the specific dimensions of these groups of families in which there are the clearest differences. Although these differences will be described in detail in the following section, it is useful here to point out that the greatest differences in this sample of families were noted regarding the distribution of power within the family, the family's mythology or use of shared denial, the use of negotiation, and the level of responsibility. Somewhat lesser (but significant) differences were noted in the nature of family coalitions, permeability, and amount of conflict.

These data demonstrate that families selected on the basis of certain shared demographic characteristics vary significantly across a range of family competence and that this variation is more marked in some dimensions of family structure and function than it is in others. The differences can be illustrated most clearly by a comparison of families rated as most and least functional.

COMPARISON OF MOST AND LEAST COMPETENT FAMILIES

Several methods will be used to illustrate the differences in families at different levels of overall family competence. We shall describe the rating scale differences and report demographic and historical differences between the two groups of families.

---

*The subscales measure power, coalitions, closeness, mythology, negotiation, autonomy, responsibility, invasiveness, permeability, range of feelings, mood, conflict, and empathy. See Appendix A for the scales themselves.

TABLE 1

Mean Beavers-Timberlawn Subscale Scores*

	Total Sample	Most Competent	Least Competent	t^{**}	df	p
	N = 18	N = 5	N = 5			
Power	3.1	1.8	4.5	9.4	8	<.005
Coalitions	2.2	1.4	3.3	3.62	4	<.025
Closeness	1.9	1.3	2.4	5.78	4	<.005
Mythology	2.8	1.9	4.0	3.74	5	<.01
Negotiation	3.5	2.0	4.7	9.80	4	<.005
Self-Disclosure	2.8	1.9	3.6	3.69	8	<.005
Responsibility	2.7	1.8	4.0	7.72	8	<.005
Invasiveness	1.9	1.5	2.4	2.43	8	<.025
Permeability	3.0	1.9	3.8	4.39	8	<.005
Expressiveness	2.9	2.0	3.6	2.17	8	N.S.
Mood	1.9	1.3	2.7	2.71	4	<.05
Conflict	2.7	1.6	3.5	2.74	8	<.025
Empathy	3.3	2.2	4.1	4.36	8	<.005

*Scales rearranged so that all go in the same direction.
**One-tailed tests.

Rating Scale Comparisons

Those families rated as most competent demonstrated shared parental leadership. This pattern was in contrast to the least competent families, in which either one parent was extremely dominant and controlling or there was overt parental conflict and no clear authority. The parental coalitions were rated as moderately strong in the most competent families and weak in the least competent families. The members of the most competent families shared a great deal of closeness, but maintained clear ego boundaries. In the least competent families there was greater interpersonal distance, although with clear evidence of individuation of family members.

The individuals comprising the two groups of families completed the Family Characteristics Inventory, a 50-item paper-and-pencil test.*

---

*See Appendix C

There were no differences between the best functioning and least well-functioning families. It is not surprising, therefore, that the three raters who independently scored the 50-minute family interactional testing scored the families differently on the Family Mythology Subscale. This subscale is designed to measure whether a family's shared attitude about itself is congruent with the rater's impression of the family and it is interpreted as a measure of the family's use of shared denial. The most competent families were seen by the raters much as they saw themselves, that is, as having many strengths. The least competent families were seen as denying their obvious pain and inefficiency.

The well-functioning families relied on the processes of negotiation in solving problems, and they dealt with experimental problems efficiently, in contrast to the inefficient problem-solving of the least well-functioning families.

The two groups of families were quite different in regard to variables thought to influence the development of individual autonomy. The most competent families were both moderately clear in their communications and highly responsive to each other. Individuals accepted responsibility for their own feelings, thoughts, and behaviors; invasions (speaking for each other or "mind-reading") were rare. In contrast, the least competent families were most often rated as somewhat vague in their communications and frequently unresponsive to each other. There was much blaming of each other, but few invasions.

These two groups of families also managed their feelings very differently. The most competent families were open with each other despite the discomfort within the family that such open expressiveness might arouse. The least competent families seemed vague or unable to express feelings, creating a baseline mood of either mere politeness or overt hostility, which was very different from the warmth, affection, and humor seen in the most competent families. There was little chronic conflict in the competent families, in contrast to the evidence of chronic conflict which impaired the functioning of the least competent families. The well-functioning families demonstrated moderate levels of empathic responsiveness, whereas there was a clear absence of demonstrable empathy in the least competent families.

These differences in the raters' perceptions of the internal milieu of the two groups of families are clear. When viewed as system characteristics, these differences suggest very different environments for finding both emotional support for a strong sense of connectedness and encouragement for separateness and autonomy. However, these perceptions grow out of a very limited observation: 50 minutes of videotaped family interaction of the ten families. The demographic and historical data are a second important source of information.

Demographic and Historical Differences

The two groups of families differed in regard to critical economic variables. These differences may be illustrated in several ways. The most competent families had greater total family income, which ranged from $10,600 to $15,320, with a mean of $12,764. This is in contrast to the least competent families, whose total family income ranged from $6,600 to $14,000, with a mean of $9, 260. These are 1979 dollars; to put these findings in perspective, it should be noted that the 1978 median income for two-parent black families was $15,913, and if both parents were employed outside the home, $22,125.[1]

The importance of these differences in total family income is given emphasis when total family income is compared to national poverty levels (1979), taking into consideration family size.[2] The total family income of the most competent families ranged from $686 to $8,216 above the poverty level, with a mean of $4,024. In striking contrast, three of the five less well-functioning families had total family incomes below the poverty level for families their size. As a group they ranged from $5,680 below the poverty level to $6,588 above that level. The group mean for the five families was $4,361 *below* the poverty level.

When the figures for both total family income and its relationship to family poverty levels adjusted for family size for the total sample of 18 families are examined, a critical threshold effect is suggested. This is illustrated in Figures 4 and 5.

Mean figures for small samples must be interpreted with great caution, but these data suggest that the families rated as least competent on the basis of family videotapes are, as a group, dealing with an economic life very different from that of the most competent. They demonstrate both a broader range of income and greater mean differences in relationship to poverty levels. The fact that the eight families with intermediate ratings in global functioning have almost identical total

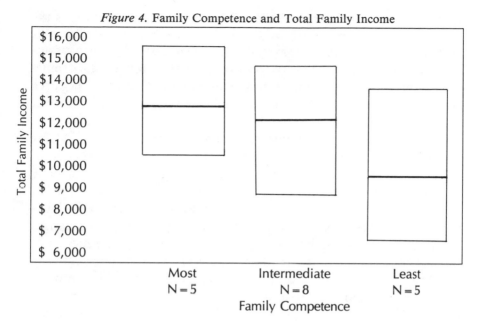

Figure 4. Family Competence and Total Family Income

Total Family Income

$16,000		
$15,000		
$14,000		
$13,000		
$12,000		
$11,000		
$10,000		
$ 9,000		
$ 8,000		
$ 7,000		
$ 6,000		

Most   Intermediate   Least
N = 5   N = 8   N = 5

Family Competence

Figure 5. Family Competence and Family Income Related to Poverty Levels

Relationship of total
Family Income to
Poverty Level

+ $9,000	
+ $7,000	
+ $5,000	
+ $3,000	
+ $1,000	
− $1,000	
− $3,000	
− $5,000	
− $7,000	

Most   Intermediate   Least
(N = 5)   (N = 8)   (N = 5)

family incomes with those of the most competent families raises the issue of the relationship of family competence to income. That this probably is not a simple linear relationship is suggested by the two families with incomes above the poverty level who were seen as least competent. Nevertheless, it is important to emphasize that each of the three families with incomes below their size-adjusted poverty levels was seen as least competent.

The differences in the economic circumstances of the best and least well-functioning families are important, and they are reflected in other indices. One father in each group was disabled and not working. The remaining four fathers in the most competent group were employed in semi-skilled occupations. Two of the fathers in the least well-functioning group were in semi-skilled jobs, and the other two were manual laborers. The fathers in both groups were, however, for the most part steadily employed—often for 10 or more years with the same employer.* The four nondisabled fathers in the best functioning families were involved with second or "moonlighting" jobs either regularly or occasionally. None of the four nondisabled fathers in the least well-functioning families reported a second job.

The wives in the two groups of families were much alike regarding employment. In each group two were full-time housewives, two were employed outside the home as domestic servants, and one was employed as a skilled worker. In both groups of families, the adolescent children often contributed some of their afterschool and summer earnings to the family income.

Fathers in both groups of families had many health problems. The five fathers in the least well-functioning families had chronic disease. Four had severe hypertension, usually with other diseases such as arthritis, migraine headaches, or peptic ulcers. The fifth father had chronic, severe renal disease and significant bilateral deafness. In the most competent families, three of the fathers were in good health. One had hypertension and diabetes mellitus, and another had coronary arteriosclerosis, a herniated lumbar disc with symptoms, and ulcerative large bowel disease that had required surgical intervention.

---

*This was true in 1979 before the worsening of the economy. Data are not available for the current occupational status of these men.

One of the mothers in each group had chronic hypertension and associated coronary artery disease. With the exception of one child with a convulsive disorder, none of the children in these ten families was known to have serious health problems.

When the focus is turned to the families' living arrangements, the findings do not discriminate the two groups. The neighborhoods in which these families live have been described (see Chapter 3). Each of the families lived in a modest home which they were buying. Two of the families in each group maintained their homes extremely well. The exteriors of these frame houses were painted and well repaired. The yards had lawns and were clean. The interiors of the homes, although modest, were clean and well furnished. There was a shared sense of family pride about their homes.

Three of the families in each group, however, had very different living circumstances. Their homes were not well tended; paint was peeling off, and windows, doors, and steps were often in poor repair. The interiors of several of these rundown houses were clean and neat, but some were sparsely furnished, dirty, and disorderly. The most striking difference, however, was the yards of these six homes, which were piled with junk and overgrown with weeds.

Although family values concerning cleanliness and order may be involved, there are modest total family income differences between the families in well-kept homes and those in poorly-kept homes (means of $10,940 and $9,560 respectively). Our sample size is too small to know whether the fact that the wife was employed outside the home was a factor in the condition of the interior of the home. In four of the six homes that were poorly kept, the wives worked outside the home, and in two of the four well-kept homes the mothers were employed.

At this point in our comparison of the most and least competent families, the demographic data underscore the importance of economic factors in discriminating the two groups. Other factors, however, may be associated with the differences between the two groups. For example, the parents in the least well-functioning families are older, less well educated, and more recently from rural areas. They are more likely to have had prior marriages and have more children.

The fathers in the most competent families have a mean age of 44 years (range 35 to 57 years), and the mothers a mean age of 39 years (range 35 to 50 years). In contrast, the fathers in the least well-functioning families have a mean age of 53 years (range 43 to 58 years), and the mothers a mean age of 48 years (range 43 to 52 years).

For eight of the ten parents in the most competent group, the current marriage was the only marriage, and the same was true of five of the ten parents in the least well-functioning group. The mean duration of the current marriage was 18 years for the better functioning group and 26 years for the least well-fuctioning group.

The better functioning families had a mean number of four children (range three to five), and the least well-functioning families had an average of 7.6 children (range three to ten). Most of the children of the former group were younger and still at home, while in the latter and older group many were out on their own.

The educational attainments of the two groups of parents were dissimilar. In the well-functioning families the fathers have a mean educational level of 11.8 years and the mothers 11.6 years. In the least well-functioning families, the fathers have a mean educational level of 8.2 years and the mothers 7.8 years.

Some of the differences in educational attainments may reflect the backgrounds of these parents and the difficulties of urbanization for individuals who are both poor and members of ethnic minorities. Dallas is frequently the destination for poor blacks migrating from the economic deprivation of rural east Texas. Seven of the ten parents from the least well-functioning families grew up in small, isolated hamlets with rural segregated school systems and came to Dallas during adolescence or young adulthood. Only three of the ten parents from the most competent families have such histories, the remainder having grown up in Dallas. Although they also attended segregated schools, the urban system was more likely to enforce the legal educational requirements. More of the fathers in the least well-functioning families recalled their early childhood and family life as grossly unstable (four of five as contrasted to one of five from the better functioning families), although there were no differences in these appraisals for the mothers.

There are marked differences in the ways in which these two groups of families interact with their environments. For example, more of the parents in the most competent families were involved in both church activities and youth-centered groups such as the PTA and Boy Scouts or Girl Scouts. Fewer of the parents from the less competent families were involved in religious activity and none were in youth-related community groups.

The differences between these two groups of families are distinct, but must be interpreted with caution because of the small sample size. Perhaps they can best be considered as descriptions that suggest hypotheses to be tested in subsequent research with larger samples.

Despite this caveat, the data suggest that ratings of global family competence in this sample can be used to describe two groups of families. The well-functioning families were significantly below the national mean for two-parent black family income, but on the average about $4,000 above the size-adjusted family poverty level. The interactional processes noted in these families are similar to those noted in middle- and upper-middle-class white families known to produce psychologically healthy children and to support the continuing emotional maturation of the parents.

The least well-functioning group of families were, as a group, about $4,000 below the size-adjusted poverty level. They were larger families with less well educated parents, and significantly more of the parents had come as young people to the city from their rural, deprived family backgrounds. The interactional processes noted in these families (which were the basis of the ratings of the two groups) are similar to those noted in middle- and upper-middle-class families known to produce more psychiatrically ill children and to serve less well as a support system for the parents.

These differences in family structure and function are, as anticipated, associated with differences in the various measures of individual functioning of the family members.

COMPARISON OF INDIVIDUALS IN MOST AND LEAST COMPETENT FAMILIES

In our earlier study of middle- and upper-middle-class white families, independent assessments of the psychological health of family members correlated with the global competence of the family. This finding was taken as partial validation of the assessment of family competence. It seemed especially important to repeat that aspect of the research with this sample of families because of the socioeconomic and ethnic differences in the two samples. If, for example, the mean level of psychological health in the members of this sample of families had no predictable relationship to assessments of their family's competence, it would appear reasonable to question the basis for the family assessments.

The instruments used were an exploratory psychiatric interview, the California Psychological Inventory, the Offer Adolescent Self-image Questionnaire, and the Shipley Hartford Vocabulary Scale and Abstraction Scale.

Exploratory Psychiatric Interview

Each parent and child was interviewed by a member of the research team (J.G.L.), a white psychiatrist trained in both adult and child psychiatry, or by T.T., a black psychiatric social worker. The interviews were carried out in the subjects' homes and were tape-recorded. The interviewers had no knowledge of the independent ratings of family competence.

The interviews were designed to obtain data useful in assessing individual social competence as judged by the capacity for work, love, and play. Work was evaluated by exploring the individual's functioning in outside employment, maintenance of the home, or school performance. Love was evaluated by exploring three groups of relationships – friends, family members, and intimates. Play was evaluated by exploring the individual's participation in leisure time activities.

The interview tapes were transcribed, de-identified, and presented to three raters (V.A.P., F.D.B., T.T.). The raters used a five-point Global Life Adaptation Scale* to quantify their impressions derived from the interview transcripts. There were 90 interviews, and the raters' scores were significantly correlated (Pearson Correlations .49–.64, $p < .01$). The raters' scores were combined for statistical purposes. Table 2 presents the comparison for the most and least competent families.

---

*See Appendix D

TABLE 2

Mean Individual Interview Ratings

Subjects	N	Mean Score	t	DF	p
Parents					
Most Competent Families	10	3.7			
Parents			2.27	18	<.025
Least Competent Families	10	2.4			
Children					
Most Competent Families	16	3.4			
Children			3.22	36	<.005
Least Competent Families	22	2.5			

As can be seen in Table 2, the parents from families independently assessed as most competent were seen, as a group, as having a better than average life adaptation, and the parents from the least competent families were rated as having a less than average life adaptation. The same was true for the children from the two groups of families. In summary, this approach to understanding the differences between the two groups of families is seen as confirming the earlier work with middle- and upper-middle-class samples.

California Psychological Inventory (CPI)

Our decision to use this instrument rather than the Minnesota Multiphasic Personality Inventory (MMPI), used in our earlier work, was based on information suggesting that the CPI had the capacity to make finer distinctions between levels of function in nonclinical samples.

We expected that members of families rated as most competent would have healthier scores on the CPI than would individuals from the least well-functioning families, but before presenting that analysis it is necessary to deal with an unanticipated finding: 35 of the 90 individuals filled out their CPIs in ways that invalidated the results. These 35 individuals were disproportionately overrepresentative of the least well-functioning families. Twenty-four of the 46 individuals from such families completed their CPIs in an invalidating manner, in contrast

to 11 of 44 individuals from better functioning families (Chi Square —
6.99, $p < .01$). Of the 55 individuals with valid CPIs, 32 were members
of either the five most competent or five least competent families. A
comparison of their mean scores is presented in Table 3.

With the exception of the Femininity (Fe) score, the average scores
for this sample fell below the mean of the norm. This finding is in agreement with other studies that indicate the CPI scores of lower-income
blacks tend to be lower than those of the standardization sample.[3] Our

TABLE 3

**Mean Scores on the California Psychological Inventory
and Membership in Most or Least Competent Families**

	Total Sample	Most Competent	Least Competent	T (OP-PA)	Prob.
	N = 55	N = 20	N = 12		
Dominance	26.11	27.65	25.67	1.32	N.S.
Capacity for Status	13.56	14.60	12.33	2.01	<.05
Sociability	21.4	23.15	20.67	1.76	<.05
Social Presence	27.84	29.65	25.33	2.33	<.025
Self-acceptance	18.27	19.6	16.83	2.19	<.025
Sense of Well Being	30.33	31.8	27.59	1.54	N.S.
Responsibility	26.00	27.95	22.67	2.70	<.01
Socialization	34.13	34.8	34.92	.008	N.S.
Self-control	29.00	28.3	28.5	.006	N.S.
Tolerance	14.13	14.8	12.25	1.30	N.S.
Good Impression	17.75	16.75	18.83	.87	N.S.
Communality	24.33	25.2	23.08	2.48	<.01
Achievement via Conformance	24.31	25.2	24.0	.659	N.S.
Achievement via Independence	13.31	14.55	11.25	2.15	<.01
Intellectual Efficiency	30.22	31.95	27.0	2.35	<.025
Psychological Mindedness	9.82	9.55	10.17	.654	N.S.
Flexibility	5.69	6.6	4.08	2.24	<.025
Femininity	20.65	20.55	22.25	1.07	N.S.

data correspond to the reports that indicate that average scores for this population are likely to be in the 40s, rather than at the standardized norm of 50. Thus, in our population higher scores are closer to the norm and, hence, healthier (with the exception of Fe, when a lower score would be close to the norm and healthier). In 14 of the 18 variables, the differences are in the predicted direction, and in 9 of the 18 the differences are statistically significant. It appears that, as a group, individuals from the more competent families are healthier (as judged by CPI scores) than individuals from the least competent families.

The CPI data suggest specifically that members of the most competent families are apt to be more self-confident and manifest greater social poise. They are more apt to enjoy social interaction and experience themselves as outgoing. These persons have a greater sense of personal worth and place higher value on hard work, duty, and consideration of others. They experience themselves as conscientious, responsible, and dependable. At the same time, these individuals are more creative and value independence of thought. They have a higher tolerance for ambiguity and are more antiauthoritarian than members of the less competent families. They also are more flexible and adaptable.

Despite the large number of invalid responses, the CPI data also support the proposition that families independently judged to be more competent contain or produce individuals who, on the average, are seen as having higher levels of psychological health.

The Offer Self-image Questionnaire
for Adolescents (OSIQ)

This instrument is a self-descriptive personality test containing 130 items designed to measure psychological adjustment in 11 areas thought to be important in the adaptation of adolescents. Thirty-three of the 43 adolescents responded with a valid questionnaire and 10 did not. These data and the comparison between the adolescents from the most and least competent families are presented in Table 4.

The most striking aspect of these findings is the marked differences of the scores between the adolescents from the most and least competent families. Although the numbers are small, the adolescents from

TABLE 4

Offer Adolescent Self-image Questionnaire Mean Scores and Membership in Most and Least Competent Families

	Total Sample N = 33	Most Competent N = 9	Least Competent N = 16	p
1. Impulse Control	45.5	52.4	39.6	<.025
2. Emotional Tone	43.9	51.0	38.5	<.05
3. Body and Self-Image	46.3	50.2	40.4	N.S.
4. Social Relations	45.6	59.7	36.5	<.005
5. Morals	44.4	48.9	40.0	N.S.
6. Sexual Attitudes	47.1	52.0	42.0	N.S.
7. Family Relations	45.5	45.8	41.9	N.S.
8. Mastery of External World	41.8	50.1	34.9	<.025
9. Vocational Goals	40.3	48.4	32.3	<.025
10. Psychopathology	42.2	53.1	37.0	<.005
11. Super Adjustment	40.0	49.5	37.5	<.05
Total Score	41.1	51.4	33.0	<.005

One-tailed difference of means tests between the most and least competent family mean. All scores are reported in their standard.

the most competent families have mean subscale scores that are close to or slightly above the mean of 50, which reflects normal functioning for adolescents. In contrast, the adolescents from the least competent families have mean subscale scores which, on the average, are 17 points below the mean and are within the pathological range.

The scores on the specific subscales indicate that, in contrast to adolescents from the least competent families, the adolescents from the most competent families experience themselves as having greater impulse control, more positive emotional tone, better social relations, greater mastery of external events, clearer vocational goals, lesser psychopathology, and superior overall adjustment.

The OSIQ data are consistent with the data from the exploratory psychiatric interviews and the CPI: Individuals comprising the most competent families achieve superior levels of overall psychological adjustment compared to individuals from the least competent families.

This is true for both the adults and the adolescents in both groups of families. The subscales of both the CPI and OSIQ suggest the specific personality dimensions in which these differences are greatest.

At this point in the analysis of differences between the members of the most and least competent families, the results are similar to those in our study of middle- and upper-middle-class families. However, we also have data that were unanticipated and different from the earlier study: the demonstration of significant differences in the results of intelligence testing between members of these two groups of families.

Shipley-Hartford Vocabulary Scale and Abstraction Scale

In the total sample of 18 families, there is a significant relationship between measures of family members' intelligence and the independently rated level of family competence ($r = -.56, p < .01$).* The comparison of the measure of intelligence for individuals from the most and least competent families is presented in Table 5.

The differences are apparent for both the parents and the children in the two groups of families (parents' IQ = 96.3 and 70.3, $t = 3.42$, $p < .005$, and children's IQ = 97.15 and 70.52, $t = 4.29$, $p < .005$).

The source of these significant differences is apparent in Table 6. One factor is that families 2 and 4 have mean family estimate of intelligence quotients much higher than the remainder of the sample (37 and

TABLE 5

Mean IQ and Family Competence

	Total Sample	Most Competent	Least Competent
N	86	23	31
Mean IQ	81.88	96.78	70.45
Standard Deviation	17.88	20.02	9.49

$t = 5.84, D.F. = 30, p < .01$

---

*The negative correlation results from the fact that lower GHP scores indicate a rating of greater family competence.

TABLE 6

Estimate of Family Intelligence and Ranked Family Competence

N	Family Competence	Number in Family	Range of IQ	Median Family IQ
1	1.5	3	66–117	91
2	1.5	5	112–125	119
3	3	5	75–87	80
4	4	5	104–120	112
5	5	5	64–94	77
6	7	3	68–97	78
7	7	7	61–114	81
8	7	3	70–103	82
9	9	4	64–115	95
10	10	4	75–85	80
11	12.5	3	74–99	84
12	12.5	4	70–89	78
13	12.5	4	77–83	79
14	12.5	6	63–76	69
15	15	10	59–76	66
16	16	3	62–78	70
17	17	5	59–90	76
18	18	7	59–93	76

30 points above the sample mean, respectively). A second factor is that families 15, 17, and 18 contain four individuals whose scores were less than 59. Omitting these two atypical families and the four individuals from the analysis reduces the differences to the point of statistical insignificance ($r = -.19$, N.S.). Despite the ability to explain differences by reference to two atypical families among those judged most competent and four individuals in the families judged least competent, a variety of interpretations are possible (including those that question the entire meaning of IQ scores for individuals not members of the broad middle-class). These interpretations will be addressed in a subsequent chapter.

In the previous sections dealing with the data from the CPI and OSIQ, it was apparent that a significant number of the tests were filled out in an invalid manner. There are significant IQ differences between the subjects who responded with valid and those with invalid tests in taking the CPI, but not the OSIQ. These are presented in Table 7.

A final issue involving the IQ scores involves their correlations with other individual measures. Fifty-five members completed valid CPIs. The correlations between IQ scores and the CPI subscales are shown in Table 8.

Although the CPI is a psychological test, it is not uncommon for some scores to show modest correlations with tests of intelligence in certain samples.[4,5] In this sample, six of the 18 subscales correlated significantly with an independent measure of intelligence. These correlations suggest that individuals in this sample with higher IQ scores also tended to describe themselves as more poised and self-confident (Sp), as having a greater sense of self-worth (Sa), as being better socialized (Cm), and as being more flexible (Fx). These correlations are modest and not surprising. Two correlations, however, are more difficult to interpret. That is, individuals in this sample with higher IQ scores also tended to describe themselves as showing *less* verbal approval for compulsive self-control (Sc), and as being *less* concerned about creating a favorable or socially desirable interpersonal impression (Gi). It may be noted on Table 3 that scores on the latter two scales, Self-control and Good Impression, while not differentiating significantly between the most competent and least competent families, also showed this same reversal pattern; that is, the more competent family members attained lower scores on these two scales than was true of members of the less competent families. While these findings are somewhat difficult to interpret, it should be noted that the correlations are low and the differences small. Thus, the more competent (and those with higher IQ

TABLE 7

Correlation Between Measure of Intelligence and California Psychological Inventory

	N	Mean IQ	S.D.
Valid	56	86.71	19.39
Invalid	30	72.87	9.72

$t = 4.41$, D.F. 86, $p < .01$

TABLE 8

Correlations Between Intelligence Quotients and California Psychological Inventory Subscales*

Subscale	r	p
Dominance	.14	N.S.
Capacity for Status	.18	N.S.
Sociability	.20	N.S.
Social Presence	.40	$< .005$
Self-acceptance	.38	$< .005$
Sense of Well Being	.09	N.S.
Responsibility	.15	N.S.
Socialization	$-.03$	N.S.
Self-control	$-.24$	$< .05$
Tolerance	$-.04$	N.S.
Good Impression	$-.29$	$< .025$
Communality	.30	$< .025$
Achievement via Conformance	$-.11$	N.S.
Achievement via Independence	.21	N.S.
Intellectual Efficiency	.13	N.S.
Psychological Mindedness	$-.07$	N.S.
Flexibility	.27	$< .05$
Femininity	$-.01$	N.S.

Note $N = 55$
*Pearson Product Moment Correlation Coefficient

scores) may not be indicating irresponsible impulsivity or a total lack of concern about forming a good impression, but merely are less concerned about these issues than are individuals of lower psychological competence and lower IQ scores.

Thirty-three adolescents completed the OSIQ. The Pearsonian correlation between the OSIQ and Shipley-Hartford IQ for those subjects was .46, $p < .005$. For the 83 subjects evaluated by an exploratory psychiatric interview, the correlation was also significant ($r = .33$, $p < .005$). These significant but modest correlations lend themselves to a number of interpretations which will be discussed in a subsequent chapter. As would be expected, the measures of psychological adjustment are significantly correlated (OSIQ and exploratory interview $r = .44$, $p <$

.01). Ten of the 18 CPI subscales correlated significantly with the Global Life Adaptation Ratings based on the exploratory interviews ($r = .23 - .43$, $p < .05$ to $< .005$). The number of adolescents with both valid CPIs and OSIQs was inadequate for statistical computations to be accomplished.

Each family member completed a Rokeach Value Survey, and family medians for both terminal and instrumental values are presented in Table 9.

For the total sample family security, happiness, a comfortable life, freedom, wisdom, and true friendship are highly ranked terminal val-

TABLE 9

Rokeach Value Survey

	Terminal Values					
	Total Sample N = 89		Most Competent N = 23		Least Competent N = 33	
	Med.	Rank	Med.	Rank	Med.	Rank
A Comfortable Life	7.1	3	10.7	12	4.3	3
An Exciting Life	10.4	12	12.8	14	7.8	5.5
A Sense of Accomplishment	11.6	14	10.8	13	9.9	10
A World of Peace	9.0	10	10.0	10	7.4	4
A World of Beauty	13.4	18	13.3	15	12.0	15
Equality	8.6	9	9.8	9	10.0	11.5
Family Security	3.8	1	5.7	4	3.0	1
Freedom	7.2	4	9.0	8	7.8	5.5
Happiness	4.6	2	4.4	2	3.4	2
Inner Harmony	13.0	16	10.3	11	12.3	16
Mature Love	9.6	11	8.0	6	8.1	7
National Security	12.9	15	15.6	18	10.6	13
Pleasure	11.3	13	13.9	16	10.0	11.5
Salvation	8.25	8	1.4	1	13.2	18
Self-respect	8.1	7	6.0	5	9.7	9
Social Recognition	13.1	17	15.3	17	12.4	17
True Friendship	8.0	6	8.8	7	9.3	8
Wisdom	7.4	5	5.0	3	10.9	14

(continued)

TABLE 9 *(continued)*

	Instrumental Values					
	Total Sample $N=89$		Most Competent $N=23$		Least Competent $N=33$	
	Med.	Rank	Med.	Rank	Med.	Rank
Ambitious	8.8	7	10.8	9.5	7.7	5
Broadminded	9.9	12.5	11.8	13.5	8.0	7
Capable	11.2	15	11.3	12	9.3	13
Cheerful	9.3	9	10.0	8	7.8	6
Clean	5.6	2	5.3	4	4.6	1
Courageous	9.4	10.5	13.7	16	8.3	8
Forgiving	6.7	4	5.3	3	6.3	2
Helpful	8.6	6	8.6	7	9.0	12
Honest	4.8	1	3.7	2	8.6	10
Imaginative	15.1	17	14.8	17	15.4	17
Independent	9.9	12.5	10.9	11	8.9	11
Intellectual	12.1	16	12.0	15	13.4	16
Logical	15.9	18	16.6	18	15.6	18
Loving	6.6	3	1.7	1	6.7	3
Obedient	10.4	14	10.8	9.5	12.8	15
Polite	9.4	10.5	11.8	13.5	10.0	14
Responsible	7.6	5	7.0	6	8.4	9
Self-controlled	9.3	8	6.4	5	6.8	4

ues. To be honest, clean, loving, forgiving, responsible, and helpful are the instrumental values most highly ranked. This ranking correlates significantly ($p < .01$) with published national norms for black, white, and poor samples.

There were significant differences in the median rankings of terminal values for the most and least competent families. The rank orders are not significantly correlated ($r = .30$, N.S.). Instrumental values are significantly alike for the two groups ($r = .77$, $p < .01$). A major difference is that, on the average, family members from the most competent families rank salvation first, and individuals from the least competent families rank it last. Although both groups rank happiness second, the least competent (and most economically deprived) families rank a comfortable life third, whereas the most competent families rank it 12th of the 18 values. Family security is ranked first by the least competent families and fourth by the most competent families. Wisdom, perhaps valued only when basic needs are achieved, is ranked third by individuals from the most competent families, but 14th of 18 by members of the least competent families.

The most competent families in this sample were more like the previously studied middle- and upper-middle-class white families in their ranking of terminal values. They correlated .79 ($p < .01$), while the least competent families rankings correlated .41 ($p < .05$). There were no differences regarding instrumental values in the correlations of these two groups of families and the previously studied sample ($r = .46$ and .45 respectively, $p < .05$).

The attempt to quantify various aspects of how families transmit value orientations regarding education, social support systems, money, religion, and orientation to the future was not successful. It was not possible to obtain a satisfactory interrater reliability using three raters who watched videotaped family interviews focusing on those areas. The raters used rating scales developed by the research team to cover the following areas: 1) clarity of value expression, 2) agreement between parents, 3) children's agreement with parents' values, 4) apparent sincerity of parental discussion, 5) degree of personalized exploration of topic, 6) amount of total family participation in discussion, and 7) family's perception of ability to control their own destiny. The raters' correlations were, for the most part, positive, but too few were statistically significant to report the data, and further work is obviously in order in this area of our interest.

SUMMARY OF FINDINGS

The first question to be raised concerns the degree of variability of structure and function found in intact, working-class black families. In our sample such families vary tremendously. Using the Continuum of Family Competence derived from the work with middle- and upper-middle-class white families, the variability ranged from families designated as most competent to those seen as least competent. This finding raises questions about the assumption that families who share broad socioeconomic characteristics are more alike than different.

The second question involves the nature of the differences seen in families designated as most competent and those rated as least competent. Differences were noted in each of the variables studied: The most competent families shared power, had stronger parental coalitions, achieved greater closeness without loss of individual ego boundaries, and solved problems efficiently using the processes of negotiation. They were clear in their communications, highly responsive to each other, open with affect, moderately empathic, and without chronic, unresolvable conflict.

The least competent families were more rigid. Either power was in the hands of one parent or there was clearly visible conflict over who had the right to decide what. They were more distant in their relationships with each other, often denying the family conflict and pain, and they neither negotiated nor solved problems efficiently. Their communications were less clear, and they were unresponsive to each other. There was more chronic conflict, and they were not empathic with each other. These differences in family structure and function were of the nature anticipated from earlier work with families at various levels of family competence.

The total family incomes were markedly different. The most competent families, as well as those intermediate between most and least competent, had a mean income of between $12,000 and $13,000 — about $4,000 above the family size-adjusted poverty level. The least competent families had a mean total family income of slightly above $9,000. These families' incomes varied from family to family, with some above and some below the poverty level. As a group, however, their mean was more than $4,000 below the family size-adjusted poverty level.

When we turn to the third question, which asks about individual variations, other important differences became apparent. The finding that members of the most competent families have, on the average, higher levels of individual psychological health than do members of least competent families is no surprise. However, we did not anticipate that parents from least competent families would be older, less well educated, and more proximate to rural roots. We also did not anticipate that they would have more children, nor that the fathers would have more chronic disease and describe greater deprivation in their families of origin. However, the finding that the parents from least competent families would be less involved with the surrounding world was anticipated on the basis that more competent families in our earlier studies had higher levels of social interaction than did less competent families.

The finding that there are significant differences in measured intelligence in the individuals from the most and least competent families was wholly unanticipated. Although these differences appear to be influenced by the atypical (for this sample) response to the intelligence testing in two of the most competent families and four of the individuals in the five least competent families, they are consistent with the educationally deprived, rural backgrounds of the parents in the least competent families. Other interpretations are, of course, possible and will be discussed in Chapter 7.

The fourth question concerns the value orientations of this sample of families. As a group they correlate significantly with norms for black, white, and poor samples. There are significant differences in the ranking of terminal values for the most and least competent families. Salvation is the value ranked highest by the most competent families and ranked lowest by the least competent families. The possible meaning of this and other differences will be discussed in Chapter 7.

The final question involves the comparison of these families with the previously studied higher-income white families. Although this will be the central focus of Chapter 6, it is clear at this point that the most competent families in both samples share similarities in structure and function.

REFERENCES

1. U.S. Bureau of the Census. *Index of Federal Programs* for Senate Committee on Budget, May, 1981.
2. U.S. Bureau of the Census, March, 1980.
3. Megargee, E. I. *The California psychological inventory handbook.* San Francisco: Jossey-Bass, Inc., 1977, p. 29.
4. Ellsworth, L. Some remarks on the characteristics of minority youngsters. In Experiment in higher education staff, *Higher education for the disadvantaged: A commentary.* East St. Louis: Southern Illinois University, 1968, 44–51.
5. Benjamin, J. A. A study of the social psychological factors related to the academic success of Negro high school students. *Dissertation Abstracts International,* 1970, *30*(8-A), 4543. (Abstract).

CHAPTER 5

Two Families

The differences noted in the most and least competent families can be augmented by more descriptively detailed presentations of representative families.* In doing so, data from all levels of observation will be used.

A VERY COMPETENT FAMILY

The Hooper family was referred to the project by another family participating in the study. Obviously interested in the study, family members demonstrated high levels of information-seeking. During initial visits with a member of the research team, they asked many questions, which ranged from the pragmatic details of data collection to issues of confidentiality. The father took the lead in this probing, seemed to respect his wife's questions, and discussed the project in detail with the children. Each member of the family became involved in the decision, but Mr. Hooper was clearly the respected leader.

The family lives in a modest frame home of about 900 square feet.

---

*The descriptions of the families are presented in disguised form in order to protect the confidentiality of the families.

The short, wooded street on which they live has the appearance of an oasis of order in a larger neighborhood verging on total disintegration. The homes on their block are generally well-maintained. Theirs is an exception. It needs extensive external repair. The yard is also the least cared for on the block and quite littered. This block is surrounded by less well-cared for homes, and the neighborhood seems dominated by a nearby housing project.

The interior of the home is modestly furnished. It is clean, but the disorder suggests that the family is an active one and that appearance of the house is not a high priority. Both parents are employed — Mr. Hooper as a construction foreman and Mrs. Hooper as a domestic. Their total family yearly income is $12,500. They have four children: Betty Jo, a 15-year-old tenth grader; Samuel, a 14-year-old eighth grader; Marietta, a sixth grader at age 11; and Joy, a six-year-old daughter enrolled in kindergarten.

Both of the parents grew up in small rural communities and completed high school in those settings. Their parents are still alive and it is clear that affectionate bonds continue to exist. Mr. Hooper and his father are self-employed, doing house repairs and minor construction. The income produced by their joint venture varies from year to year, and was $9,000 in 1979 for Mr. Hooper, an amount he considers "about average." Mrs. Hooper is employed as a maid.

The family has a benign physical health history except for Mr. Hooper's serious automobile accident that resulted in a lengthy period of disability 12 years ago.

Religion is an important part of the family's life. Both parents were raised in the same fundamental Protestant denomination, and they continue to be active in a neighborhood church. The children participate in a variety of church youth activities.

When the family is observed together either for family interactional testing or for the family interview, they show strong mutual affection. They laugh a lot and demonstrate an easy familiarity with each other. The parents share leadership in the family easily. They listen to their children, solicit their opinions, and appear respectful — but there is no doubt that together they are in charge. On several occasions Mr. Hooper lapses into a more authoritative, "teaching and preaching" role, but either seems to recover spontaneously or tolerate his wife's intervention gracefully. During such moments, however, the children become more subdued, and their nonverbal messages suggest boredom. These intervals are infrequent, but during such moments the gaiety is lost, and the family becomes more apathetic. In the presence of the interviewer, the children do not participate as spontaneously as when the family is alone for the interactional testing; the parents take over much of the responsibility for responding.

Although family members are obviously close, there is much evidence of individuality. Each person speaks clearly and seems secure in disagreeing. When the family is challenged to solve experimental problems as one part of the family interactional testing, they do so efficiently and often in the process demonstrate effective negotiating skills. Verbal clarity is high and family members are most often responsive to each other. There is little apparent blaming and no evidence of invasions or mind-reading statements.

The Hoopers seem able to express a wide range of feelings, and empathic responses to affective messages come naturally. Their shared mood is often humorous, warm, and optimistic, and there is no evidence of chronic conflict.

In responding to the task of discussing family strengths, loving and caring for each other are clearly important. They emphasize talking with each other, trying to understand what each other is feeling, and sometimes giving in to each other. In this discussion the strong religious values of the family are explicit.

The family's response to the task of completing a story in which the themes of death and dying are explicit displays some measure of the family's competence. The more affluent, white families demonstrated that a good many nonclinical families discuss death and dying openly, although only a few do so in personal terms, that is, by discussing the death of a relative or a close friend.[1] This finding is in contrast to families containing an identified patient. Such families rarely respond to the task with an open discussion of death and dying; rather, they take great pains to avoid these subjects. The Hoopers' response was to discuss death openly. During the first few minutes they discussed the story and, as a group, seemed to evaluate the evidence and then concluded that the comatose "he" in the story would die. The father commented, "The doctor's statement there was damage is a bad sign," and the mother said, "The doctor's asking the family to move to the lounge to talk with him must mean that he's going to die."

Following this focus on completing the story (their assigned task), Mr. Hooper introduced a broader dimension with, "The death of someone close happens to all of us." Mrs. Hooper responded with, "It happens in *your* family." The family went on to discuss the pain of losing someone, how much time it takes to get over it, and the emptiness it can leave in one's life. The children gradually became more active, asking questions and offering comments. The family did not discuss a relative or friend's actual death. However, the family actually has not experienced the loss of a grandparent or close relative. Throughout the 10-minute discussion, the parents balanced soliciting the children's feelings and opinions with active teaching.

In the task which involves only the parents, they are asked to discuss the "best and worst" of their relationship. Mr. and Mrs. Hooper's response emphasized the positive aspects of their relationship, but the central theme was not personal satisfaction, a sense of closeness, or their sexual relationship. Rather, their focus was on the degree of economic improvement they had attained by working together, learning how to manage money, keeping current with the bills, having a home with a "big back yard," "having what you *need* (if not everything you *want*), and watching your children do well." These issues were described as the "best" of their marriage. The "worst" involved their early days together when they did not have, or had not mastered, those skills. Throughout the discussion their emphasis was on instrumental rather than relationship processes.

During both the family interview and the family interactional testing, the Hoopers' struggle with Joy, their six-year-old, was apparent. She seemed "spoiled" and somewhat immature to the members of the research team involved in data collection. Almost six years younger than her next sibling, Joy was often the focus of the family's attention. Other times, she sought to draw attention to herself. During an interactional task, when she was chastised for not minding, she burst into tears and climbed into her mother's lap, and Mr. Hooper promised her ice cream if she would only stop crying. Each of the clinician raters of the videotape noted that her behavior was more like that of a three-year-old than a six-year-old and that her role as "baby" in the family was obviously something in which all family members participated.

Mr. Hooper is a compact, muscular man who looks younger than his 35 years. He is friendly, looks one straight in the eyes, and smiles often. He finds great satisfaction in his work, and he likes both being outside and being his own boss. His income from the business fluctuates with the weather and the seasons and, by itself, does not produce enough to sustain the family at their current level. It is the only type of work that Mr. Hooper has ever done. When there is no work or during one or two weekends each month, he meets old friends to shoot pool and have a few beers. He indicates that his wife does not mind these several days or so each month that are his to do with as he will — "She thinks it's all right as long as it's not too much." The remainder of his free time is spent with the family — barbecuing, visiting with relatives, and fishing and hunting with his son.

In discussing his marriage, Mr. Hooper emphasizes the ways in which his wife's characteristics have contributed to the stability of their relationship. He was attracted by her intelligence, her looks, and her personality — particularly the fact that she wasn't "wild." He perceives her as extremely likable — and indicates that everyone who knows her "really likes her." He says their sexual relationship is a good one. Currently they have intercourse about twice a week, and their physical spontaneity was increased when she had her "tubes tied" after Joy's birth. Occasionally they become less involved with each other sexually — usually following a disagreement about money. "You'd be surprised how your financial status in the home affects your romantic life . . . because a woman, if they, if something is bugging them or something, they're just not all there, you know. . . ."

Mr. Hooper believes that their shared religious beliefs and practices are important to their relationship. The church is one of the first places they would turn to if they had problems they couldn't solve themselves. Their other major support system is their extended family — parents, siblings, and cousins.

He describes his children with obvious pride, emphasizing Samuel's reliability, Betty Jo's academic achievements and "flowery" temperament, Marietta's quiet competence, and Joy's energy and excitement.

Mr. Hooper describes himself as interested primarily in his family. Most of his sense of satisfaction comes from providing for them. He feels successful because his wife is happy and his children are doing well. The support provided by his religious beliefs is important to him. He ranks wisdom, happiness, freedom, and salvation as primary values.

At a different level, he appears to experience himself as a man of action rather than contemplation. He likes to work with his hands, to make things or grow things. Mr. Hooper is not fettered by anxiety, depression, or other symptoms suggesting psychiatric difficulty. His CPI subscales are within normal limits. In summary, Mr. Hooper is seen as functioning at a high level of psychological adaptation.

Mrs. Hooper is a robust woman who seems open, spontaneous, and direct. She works three days a week as a domestic servant, and this time is split among several affluent white families across town. It takes her an hour to go each way on various buses. She finds the work boring, but has established a routine with each family and derives a sense of autonomy in that the routine minimizes the amount of instruction she receives. "It's like working for yourself, 'cause they don't tell you what to do." Earlier in her life she had worked on an assembly line, but did not like the long hours and extremely monotonous tasks. When not at her job, Mrs. Hooper enjoys sewing, particularly making clothes for her girls. She has little free time, but emphasizes that religion and her extended family play a central role in her life. She enjoys watching certain television shows with her husband.

Mrs. Hooper describes her husband and their marriage in positive terms. She sees him as steady, reliable, and a consistent provider. His interest and participation in religious activities are pleasing to her. She feels that he has "settled into" the role of husband and father over the years, but suggests that it took real effort on her part to help him do so. A crucial issue for her is how much she can push him — when she goes too far he retreats or gets mad.

Although she enjoys their twice weekly sexual intercourse, she says that he would like it to be more frequent, but she is often tired. Her work is arranged so she gets home at 3 p.m. and must then clean her own home and cook. After dinner and some television she is ready for sleep and sometimes uninterested in sex. On the other hand, when she is distressed about something, he listens, and she appreciates his availability.

Although she describes him as a good father, she feels the major responsibility for the day-to-day aspects of childrearing.

The marital relationship for her is a good one, on balance, and most of the time she feels fortunate, but she wishes it were different in some ways. In this regard she rationalizes that he works hard and she can't expect everything she wants from him. Her tendency to search for explanations or rationalizations is also apparent in her thoughts about their economic circumstances. "Not everyone can be doctors, lawyers, and bankers—some of us must do other kinds of work." Her religious beliefs augment her search for satisfaction under far from optimal circumstances, and she expresses clearly her feeling that the present is much better than the past and that the future, both in this world and that which follows, promises even more.

Mrs. Hooper worries about, but is pleased with, her children's development. She describes each of them in positive ways that are very similar to her husband's descriptions. She is closest to Betty Jo and thinks that is because they are so much alike. "You can't get people to be exactly the way you want them to be. We learned to accept the good part and the bad part of each other—so, then, we want our kids to be like that—you learn to accept those things in each other and learn to grow together. So we try to raise our kids right so they can understand life. Life won't always be easy, but they can work at it."

Mrs. Hooper's perception of herself is positive—"basically, I'm good," she says, and her sincerity is obvious. Treating people well and helping people are part of the core of her life. When asked what she would like most to change about herself, she said, laughingly, "Well, my husband says I talk too much; I don't know, I may not change anything."

Mrs. Hooper has occasional periods of depression that last a day or two and usually seem related to real problems—"like money." Sometimes she deals with it herself, but often talks with her husband or her mother or mother-in-law. She also has a "talking relationship" with the woman she works for on Fridays. They discuss problems with each other, and Mrs. Hooper states simply, "We're close, and it helps." However, these "blues" are the exception to the usual way in which she experiences herself, and most of the time she feels competent, good, and in charge of her life.

At 15, Betty Jo is a tenth grader at a highly competitive magnet school. She wants to be a nurse and makes As and Bs. She is very popular, is actively involved in athletics, and has started dating. She feels very close to her mother and talks with her about personal issues. She also feels close to Samuel, but less so with her father and sisters. She experiences herself as bright and goal-oriented. The interviewer was impressed with her poise, physical attractiveness, and ability to express herself with both clarity and complexity.

Samuel is a handsome, athletic-looking 14-year-old who relates well to the interviewer. He is candid in sharing his dislike of school, but continues by making Cs, only because of parental expectations. He is enthusiastically involved in organized school athletics. Samuel is open about his occasional misbehavior, which has resulted in visits to the principal. He does, however, emphasize his successful efforts to avoid illicit drug use, "a bad scene." He has a girlfriend, they have sexual intercourse, and he acknowledges heterosexual experiences starting at age 13.

Samuel has a broad circle of friends and several with whom he is very close. He also feels close to his parents, and it is clear that his relationship with his mother has been very important to him. He sees her as the major disciplinarian, but she is easier for him to talk to than his father. At the same time, he sees himself as more like his father — a person able to get along well with people, popular, but having quite a temper. The interviewer perceived a struggle with conflicting sets of feelings arising out of a developmental transition: the need to be a man who is independent, even tough, and the need to feel close to his mother.

Marietta is a quiet 11-year-old. She is affectionate and, like her older sister and brother, feels closer to her mother. In fact, she is a little scared of her father because "he has a temper." She quickly undoes this statement by reminding the interviewer of how hard he works and how tired he gets. She is in the sixth grade and makes good grades, although "not as good as Betty Jo's." It is clear that she feels the impetus for making good grades comes from her mother.

Marietta has many friends, but dislikes boys. She is particularly fond of her younger sister whom she "looks after" much of the time. She impressed the interviewer as a normal prepubertal youngster who was open and warm.

Joy has just turned six and is shy with strangers. She is babied by other members of the family, gets her own way, and is often the center of attention. She is affectionate in a physical way, often touching, holding onto, or climbing on another member of the family. The interviewer felt that she is essentially a healthy six-year-old, although immature for her age.

The Hooper family was rated on the basis of the family interactional testing as a very competent family by the independent raters. The data regarding individual family members, including the exploratory interviews, CPIs, and OSIQs, demonstrated high levels of individual competence or psychological health.

The family shares a number of characteristics with other well-functioning families. Such families differ in style and on the surface appear to be very different, but in relating to each other, their shared affection, strong parental leadership, clear communication, and efficient problem-solving are evident. The Hoopers' emphasis on athletics, family cookouts, and involvement with their extended family are matters of style that distinguish them from the other competent families.

However, the Hoopers are not without problems: The parents do not communicate about intimate feelings and thoughts, their sexual relationship is not completely satisfactory to either of them, and Mrs. Hooper seems to bear the heavier burden of the day-to-day living. Also, Samuel's marginal tolerance of academic pursuits and Joy's role as the family baby are less than optimal.

Throughout the research team's contacts with the family, several themes emerged: The importance of the family, the support and structure provided by their religious beliefs and activities, and the capacity to determine their future—through work and education—are paramount. These values have seen them through some tough times, sustained them in a daily life that is only marginal financially, and facilitated a future orientation that contains promise and hope.

A CLEARLY DYSFUNCTIONAL FAMILY

The Bradley family was referred to the researchers by another family participating in the study. From the start, their attitude toward the study was a curious combination of apparently friendly interest and, at other times, a high level of guardedness. In all the researchers' contacts with the family Mr. Bradley took charge, often making decisions without involving other family members, but frequently there was nonverbal opposition from his wife and son. His decisions seemed to be the law, however, and he was never challenged in an open, verbal way.

The Bradleys live in a lower-middle-class neighborhood. Their house is brick and frame and well-maintained. The yard is well-groomed, and there are shrubs and flowers. The interior of the 1,500 square foot home is neat and furnished well. Throughout the neighborhood there is an air of pride in ownership.

Mr. Bradley has worked as a hospital orderly until recent months. He is currently on a disability allowance for a serious, chronic disease, for which he requires treatments three times each week. Mrs. Bradley is employed as a full-time domestic servant by one family. She is considering applying for disability also, citing her arthritis and "nerves" as the reasons. Her salary and her husband's disability allowance result in an annual income of $14,000, which is only slightly less than their total income prior to his disability. Their household includes Harold, their 16-year-old son and Mary Lee, the 6-year-old child of their unmarried daughter Beth, 22, who lives out of state.

Mr. Bradley was born the last child in a large rural family. His mother died soon after, and his father when he was a teenager. He did not feel close to anyone in his family and does not stay in touch with his siblings. He has always felt like a loner. He completed the tenth grade and left school to go to work. A few years later he joined the Navy and remained in military service for four years.

Mrs. Bradley, the sixth of seven children, grew up in a small town in east Texas where her father was a laborer. Both of her parents died after she was grown and, with the exception of two of her sisters, she has little contact with her family of origin. She quit school after the tenth grade in order to get married. This early marriage lasted several years and terminated in divorce.

Although each member of this family seems reasonably intact and goal-directed during individual contacts, the family is disorganized and ineffectual as a group. During both the family interactional testing and the exploratory family interview, Mr. Bradley controlled and dominated the family discussions, appearing completely impervious to messages from other family members. An example of this manner occurred in the first videotaped family task, in which the family is asked to discuss their family's strengths. The audiotaped instructions inform them that they have ten minutes in which to complete the discussion. Mr. Bradley misinterpreted this to mean they should wait ten minutes to begin. Harold corrected him and said they should start. Mr. Bradley stared at him and said, "We'll wait." Mrs. Bradley shook her head as if to say, "Here we go again," lit a cigarette, and turned her back to the family. After a tense and silent eight minutes, in which each family member stared into the distance, Mr. Bradley yelled to the researcher, who was in another room, "When do we start?" Receiving a "go ahead," he announced that the strength of their family was that each family member's problems became problems for the whole family. Mrs. Bradley said she had a problem right now. There was no response, and the family fell silent until the end of the time alloted for the task.

In the task requiring the family to complete an audiotaped story involving an explicit death and dying theme, the family never engaged the task. Rather, the father focused his attention on the girl in the vignette who was crying. He talked at length about whether or not she was on drugs, and then launched into a monologue about the evils of drugs. The mother once again turned her back on the family, and the 16-year-old son, Harold's, efforts to clarify the nature of the task did not interrupt his father's monologue. After a few minutes, the other family members adopted postures of resignation, the monologue went on until the ten minutes expired.

During the marital section of the taping, Mr. Bradley started by saying that the best of their marriage was the day they got married because he "didn't think it would last." His wife shrugged, and he then said that their best times were when they went to the movies together. After silence that was painful to the beholders, she finally commented that the best part of their marriage was that they hadn't allowed anyone to influence their relationship. "You've got to be strong to survive a marriage," she commented, and there was no answer. Throughout this section neither responded to the other's comments. Rather, each spouse made an occasional statement which was followed by a lengthy silence.

In the section in which the family is asked to discuss closeness in their family, there was very little discussion. Mr. Bradley said he was closer to his granddaughter than "anyone in the world," and Harold said he felt the same way about his mother. When the family was asked to plan something together, the father picked up his Bible and began quizzing Harold on the meaning of certain passages. Once again, Harold clarified the task, but had no impact on his father who continued with his quiz.

Throughout the entire family testing, there was a strange and difficult-to-follow quality. The family members did not interact — Mr. Bradley dominated the famiy with his talk, stares, and failure to respond to their attempted interventions. The effect was one of tenuously controlled disorganization, absence of an effective marital coalition, and totally inefficient problem-solving. The family failed to develop a shared focus of attention, and Mr. Bradley frequently invaded other family members' boundaries by telling them what they thought or felt. Most expressions of affect by other family members were nonverbal — facial expressions, body movements, and postural messages — and they communicated anger, resignation, and hopelessness directed at the father. At times, family members would get up and leave the room, leaving Mr. Bradley alone in front of the camera.

The father is a prim and precise man who relates to the interviewer with considerable caution. He avoids discussing certain subjects — his health status and the whereabouts of his daughter, for example. Much of his discussion of his life centers about his work experience. He started working when he was 12 years old. For the past ten years he has been a hospital orderly until his employment ended with his recent disability. Currently he occupies himself about the house and yard. He describes no recreational interests or activities, although he is trying to interest himself in a hobby. His church is an important part of his life; recently he was elected deacon and is very proud of the framed certificate which hangs on the livingroom wall.

He describes meeting his wife after his military service and marrying her after a brief acquaintance. In describing his wife he focused almost exlcusively on two traits — that she was truthful and a good mother. Although he acknowledges that his disease influences their sexual relationship, he says that it is "normal" for a couple who have been married 26 years. Mr. Bradley described his wife in only the barest superficialities, a characteristic that typified the entire research contact with him.

In discussing his children, the interviewer touched the only bit of affect elicited from Mr. Bradley. He described his son as a "mother's child" and had little else to say about him. However, when describing his absent daughter, Beth, he became briefly distraught and tears were obvious. He said they had been "very close" during earlier years, but he refused to discuss her current life situation.

Mr. Bradley described himself as an "average man" who enjoys his family, fixing up his house, and keeping his yard neat. If he could change anything about his life, he would have more education. This part of the interview again demonstrated Mr. Bradley's tendency to stay on the surface of things, to describe himself and others briefly and in superficial terms. His concern with order, precision, propriety, and confidentiality were obvious.

Mrs. Bradley describes her early life in positive terms, but the rigidity of her family of origin caused her to leave home to marry when she was 15. When her marriage failed she went to work at a cafe and lived with a sister. "I stayed off the streets." She recalls that Mr. Bradley asked her to marry him the first night they met and that she accepted; they married several days later.

Mrs. Bradley has been a servant five days a week for the same family for 11 years. Recently, because of her husband's illness and her "nerves" and arthritis she has cut back to two days a week. Religion is the center of her life, and she is active in a number of church activities. Her family, a relationship with a nearby sister, her home, her work, and the church make up for her personal life.

Mrs. Bradley describes her husband as a good-hearted man whom people take advantage of and mistreat. His strong work orientation dominated their life prior to his illness. She indicates that he always had two or three jobs and was home very little. She is more open than he about his illness and its impact on their lives. She feels that he is getting "mean" with his illness and that she is "about to go crazy."

There has been little open affection or communication in their marriage. "He don't tell you he loves you," she said. On special occasions he may give her a card that has "nice thoughts" on it, but that is the extent of his demonstrativeness. He has always made all the decisions for the family — "nobody can tell him anything," she said with a sigh.

In describing her children, Mrs. Bradley becomes clearly moved. Her daughter, Beth, age 22, is the source of much worry. She is the mother of six-year-old Mary Lee. Mrs. Bradley resists discussing her other than to say that she is emotionally distant like her father, to whom she has always been close. Mrs. Bradley feels closest to Harold, and she is proud of his musical ability. He is described as "good hearted," but "not too strong in some things." "People," she said, "can influence Harold too easily." It was, however, difficult for the interviewer to get her to be specific about these concerns.

Mrs. Bradley describes herself as a person who likes to be at home or at church. She likes helping people, but is wary about relationships with outsiders. She smokes incessantly and wishes she had the willpower to stop. The interviewer's attempts to explore her self-system were not successful. She presents herself in bland and superficial terms. She is patently tense, hyperactive, and jumps from subject to subject without exploring any one subject in any depth. The researchers were unable to learn any details about Beth except that she lives out of the state.

Harold also is tense and hyperactive and relates in a guarded way to the interviewer. He describes himself as a good B and C student, but his primary interest is music. He plays the violin at school and church functions. He indicates that because he takes lessons he does not have an outside job or participate in extracurricular actitivities. Harold feels that he is more popular with his teachers than with other students. He indicates that he is interested in girls, but does not elaborate.

Harold feels closest to his mother and an aunt who lives nearby with whom he can discuss anything he wishes. He has a more distant relationship with his father who "tries to block everything out," making him relatively inaccessible.

He has a chronic medical condition which is well controlled by the medication he takes. However, he did not give this information to the research team; rather, his father did.

Mary Lee, the six-year-old granddaughter, is in many ways the center of her grandparents' lives. She is a bright and energetic youngster, whose relationship with Harold is becoming increasingly conflicted. "She was cute when she was a baby, but now she's a lot of trouble."

The Bradley family is rated as severely dysfunctional, bordering on chaos. This level of functioning could not be easily inferred from the individual interviews because each of the three persons interviewed was able to maintain the focus on the surface. However, the oberserver can note signs of severe dysfunction: Mr. Bradley's intense need to maintain control, his imperviousness to others, the absence of warmth or closeness among family members, his gross inefficiency in problem-solving, the subjects that are taboo in the family discussions, the barely muted depression and anger, the absence of a strong parental coalition. Such signs point to the presence of severe pain and conflict within the family, which are denied as family members individually insist that they have a strong family.

It is possible, however, to speculate that the severe family dysfunction represents regression under stress. The Bradley family has functioned around Mr. Bradley's dominance for many years and, because of his serious disease and need for treatments, the family has regressed and denial and fragmentation have increased. The family seems unable to discuss the implications of Mr. Bradley's disease openly, and in their family interactional task to complete the vignette about death and dying he maintained a focus on drug abuse, a topic that was irrelevant to the stimulus material or their personal situation.

The Bradleys are a family with an uncertain, possibly tragic, immediate future. Mr. Bradley's serious disease strikes at the very family member who manages the family, albeit with a heavy and controlling hand. It is questionable whether either Mrs. Bradley or Harold has the strength the future may require.

These two families, the Hoopers and the Bradleys, are very different across a broad range of variables, and it is not difficult to understand that, both in the emotional support that grows out of human connectedness and in the facilitation of individual autonomy, membership in these two families has very different impact.

REFERENCES

1 . Lewis, J. M., Beavers, W. R., Gossett, J. T., & Phillips, V. A. *No single thread: Psychological health in family systems.* New York: Brunner/Mazel, 1976.

CHAPTER 6

Comparison of Competent Families From Different Socioeconomic Contexts

The similarities and differences between the most competent black families in this study and the most competent middle- and upper-middle-class white families studied earlier are critical to the question posed by one of our research hypotheses. That hypothesis stated that the most competent black working-class families would require a basic pattern of dominance by one parent, rather than the more equal power shared by the parents in the most competent affluent families. The dominant-submissive organizational structure was an expected system change to more rigidity under the stress of socioeconomic circumstances. Thus, the family structure is seen as responding to its context. It is important to emphasize that, although families contribute to the context, for a particular family this influence is usually less than the impact of the context on the family.

Before examining in some detail the ways in which these two groups of well-functioning families are alike and the ways in which they are different, several issues need clarification. The first involves the differences between the two studies. These include: 1) an interval of 12 years separated the two studies; 2) the sample for the earlier study was obtained through a single source, a large Protestant church, whereas the sample for the second study was obtained from three sources: a ministerial alliance, a high school student council, and referral from participating families; 3) the families in this study were paid a $50 honorarium for participating, and there was no honorarium for the earlier sample; 4) all the data were collected in the families' homes in this study, whereas some of the data (the family interviews and inter-actional testing) were collected at the Timberlawn Research Foundation in the earlier study; 5) in some instances, different and/or additional instruments were used for data collection in this study; and 6) data were collected by different members of the research team in each of the two studies.

A second issue requiring clarification involves the extent of the socio-economic differences between these two groups of well-functioning families. The five black families rated as most competent had total family incomes of from $10,600 to $15,320, with a mean of $12,764. With an average of four children (range three to five), this placed them above the family size-adjusted poverty level but considerably below the national median income for two-parent black families and far below the median income for two-parent families in which both parents work. Two of the families lived in modest but well-maintained homes and three lived in poorly maintained homes.

Four of the fathers were employed in semi-skilled jobs, and one was disabled. These working four had second part-time jobs. Two of the mothers were at home full-time, and three were employed outside the home—two as domestic servants and one as a skilled worker. The health status of two of the fathers and one of the mothers was impaired by hypertension and its sequelae. The fathers had a mean age of 44 years, and the mothers of 39 years. The parents had, on the average, high school educations and were active in church and child-related organizations.

The six highly competent white families lived in very different socio-economic circumstances. Although income data were not obtained in the original study, the six families are all classified by the Hollingshead Four Factor Index of Socioeconomic Status at Levels I and II. All of the fathers were college graduates; two were presidents of small companies, two were independent professionals, one was an executive in a major construction firm, and one was the principal of a large high school. Four of the mothers were college graduates and the other two had completed two years of college. Five of the mothers were full-time in the home and one was a full-time professional employee.

All six families lived in affluent suburbs in large, well-maintained brick homes. They had two, and in some instances, three cars. Each family had some form of savings and retirement programs.

The fathers ranged in age from 31 to 51 years (average 42 years), and the mothers from 32 to 50 years (average 39 years). The families contained from two to four children (average three children), and in each family the oldest child was an adolescent. No other relatives lived with any of these six families.

COMPARISON OF THE TWO GROUPS OF FAMILIES

As can be noted, the socioeconomic circumstances of these two groups of families are very different. Despite such differences, the families look much alike when their relationship processes are studied in family interactional testing. Table 10 presents the Beavers-Timberlawn subscale scores for the two samples and the two groups rated as most competent.

Although there are some modest differences between the scores for the two samples, there are no differences in the scores for the families seen as most competent. The working-class black families demonstrate interactional processes that are similar to those of the earlier studied, more affluent families. They are characterized by:

1) A strong parental coalition.
2) Parents who share power and provide joint leadership to the family.
3) Closeness and individuation within the family.
4) Recognition and acceptance of the family's strengths and weaknesses.
5) Efficient task performance.
6) Skills in negotiation.
7) Clear expression of thoughts and feelings.
8) Individual sense of responsibility.
9) Few invasions or "mind-reading."
10) Openness to each other's communication.
11) Direct expression of a wide range of feelings.
12) A prevailing mood that is warm, affectionate, and optimistic.
13) No chronic, seemingly unresolvable family conflict.
14) Empathic responsiveness to each other.

TABLE 10

**Comparison of Beavers-Timberlawn Subscale Scores for the
Two Groups of Families†**

	Total Sample		Most Competent	
	Working-Class Black	Upper-Middle-Class White	Working-Class Black	Upper-Middle-Class White
Number	18	33	5	6
Structure	3.1	***2.1	1.8	2.1
Coalition	2.2	2.0	1.4	1.5
Closeness	1.9	***2.5	1.3	1.6
Mythology	2.8	**2.0	1.9	1.9
Negotiation	3.5	***2.7	2.0	1.8
Clarity	2.8	2.7	1.9	2.0
Responsibility	2.7	2.3	1.8	1.9
Invasiveness	1.9	2.0	1.5	1.4
Permeability	3.0	3.0	1.9	1.8
Expressive-ness	2.9	2.9	2.0	2.4
Feeling Tone	1.9	1.9	1.3	1.5
Conflict	2.7	*2.1	1.6	2.1
Empathy	3.3	***2.9	2.2	2.1

†Some scale scores reversed so that all scales are in the same direction.
t tests difference of means: ***$p < .01$; **$p < .02$; $p < .05$
All other differences are N.S.

In addition to the family interactional testing, each of the families in this sample was interviewed using a semi-structured format. The interview explored the family's attitude regarding money, religion, education, support systems, and expectations for the future. The resulting videotapes were analyzed by a member of the research team (C.T.). This interview format was not used in the earlier study. In most instances, however, the same topics were explored in the six hours of family interviews the earlier sample underwent.

The most competent families in the lower income sample were similar in their attitudes about these important topics. Despite marginal economic circumstances, concerns about money did not dominate their discussions. Rather, they thought it was important to manage their money so as to pay bills and stay out of debt, but also to obtain some pleasure from the use of money. Budgeting was important for most of these families, and trying to accumulate a savings was important for several families. The children participated in discussions about money in all of the families. The more affluent families from the earlier study also dealt with money in a matter-of-fact way. The necessity to manage, plan, budget, and, at times, do without something they wanted was equally clear in this group. However, the differences in what one went without were striking. For the affluent families this most frequently involved special or luxury items — a new and expensive car before the old one had worn out, or a particular kind of costly vacation. For the working-class families in this sample, the "wants" were much more basic — a newer car because the old one had quit running, the opportunity to visit relatives living several hundred miles away, or something else far less costly than the possibilities discussed by the more affluent families.

Religious beliefs and activities were at the center of the most competent working-class families' lives. The themes emerging in their discussions involved the importance of the church in raising children, providing moral guidelines, and augmenting the cohesiveness of the family unit. The more affluent families demonstrated more variation in the role that religion played in their lives. For several families it occupied the same central position as with all of the working-class families. More often, however, religion was considered important and church attended with regularity, but it was not a central, organizing aspect of family life.

Education was important to all of the most competent families in both samples. For the more affluent group, college and, perhaps, professional or graduate school were taken for granted. "John wants to be a lawyer," or "Jean wants to get a doctorate in anthropology and do field work in Africa" were reflections of typical aspirations. For the working-class families, education, while of at least equal importance, had less extensive goals. For these families going to college was a way of preparing oneself for a better job and, subsequently, for a better standard of living. The aspirations and expectations were positive and strongly cathected, but more modest.

Both groups of families had sources of support outside the nuclear family. The extended family, close friends, and a variety of organizations were mentioned routinely. The working-class families, however, noted the church as a primary support system more frequently.

Finally, both groups of families were intense and optimistic towards the future. Although some parents in both groups articulated the bittersweet nature of the children's growing up and leaving, in the same breath they commented on the anticipated pleasure of lessened parental responsibility and the opportunity to pursue other interests. They were neither apprehensive nor tentative as they looked ahead.

In summary, when viewing these two groups of highly competent families from the perspective of observations of the family system, the relationship processes are strikingly alike. That which appears to "work best"* for middle- and upper-middle-class white families also appears to "work best" for working-class black families.

Another level of observation of the family reflects individual family members' perceptions. These observations are filtered through the perceptual and interpretive processes of the individual family members, and much that is of value in understanding the family can be obtained. Also, in our earlier work such individually-based family data complemented the observations of the total family system.

The members of both samples of competent families perceived their families in much the same way as did members of the research team. For these families that meant, of course, an acknowledgment that the family was strong, competent, or healthy. It was also clear that individuals valued their families tremendously. They felt fortunate to be part of and contribute to such families. This did not interfere, however, with their ability to acknowledge problems and conflicts. There was no apparent need to experience the family as perfect in any way.

COMPARISONS OF THE INDIVIDUALS IN THE TWO GROUPS OF FAMILIES

The individuals who comprised both groups of families shared certain characteristics but were different in other ways. With a few exceptions they were evaluated as functioning at average or higher levels of

---

*"Work best" is, of course, considered from the viewpoint of the value judgments underlying the Continuum of Family Competence as discussed in Chapter 1.

psychological health. The individual exploratory interviews were evaluated in a different way in the two studies. In the initial study raters used the Luborsky Health-Sickness Rating Scale, and each individual received a rating from 0 to 100. Three of the 30 individuals (one parent and two children) received ratings suggesting of symptomatic states, none of which were of the nature of a major psychiatric syndrome. The other 27 individuals were rated as functioning well. In the second study, clinicians rated the individual interview transcripts on a 5-point scale of current functioning. Three of the 20 individuals (two parents and one child) were rated as functioning below average levels of psychological health. These approaches to the evaluation of psychological functioning are, at best, rough approximations, but these are greater prevalences of rated psychological health than were found in individuals comprising families scored as less competent.

With comparably rare exceptions, both groups of family members experienced themselves in positive ways. Two of the mothers in the working-class families described periods of mild to moderate depression, generally lasting several days and occurring several times a year. These women had not sought treatment, and both described the helpful effect of talking with their husbands. Several of the adolescents described periods of anxiety related to actual events. Several of the parents described what appeared to be significant depressive episodes some years earlier, and these were related to job loss or disability from illness or accident. At the present time, however, both the adults and children seemed to have clear, cohesive, and positive images of themselves.

Despite the socioeconomic differences in the lives of these two groups of individuals, their value orientations were very much alike. Salvation, family security, happiness, self-respect, and wisdom were the five highest ranked terminal values on the Rokeach Value Survey for both groups. In fact, only one of the 18 terminal values was ranked differently by the two groups in a way that was statistically significant. This involved the value "a sense of accomplishment," which was ranked sixth by the members of the more affluent families and 13th by members of the working-class families.

The two groups of families were also much alike in their rankings of instrumental values. Honest, loving, and forgiving were the highest ranked values for both groups of family members. There were only two instrumental values that were ranked so differently as to be statistically significant. The members of working-class families ranked "logical" as the 18th or least important value, whereas members of the more affluent families ranked it tenth. The former group ranked the value "clean" as fourth and the latter group ranked it 14th.

Fathers

When the focus is changed from the total family system to the individuals comprising the two groups of families, anticipated differences become clear. The fathers in the middle- and upper-middle-class white families had attained high levels of vocational success, both in terms of status and economic rewards. They derived a great deal of satisfaction from their jobs. Five of the six men received little direct supervision in their work, and they relished the autonomy and leadership their jobs provided. Major job satisfactions involved persuading and helping employees to succeed. Four of the six men would want the same job if they "had to do it all over again." One of the men regretted his choice of vocation, feeling that both the personal and financial rewards would have been greater in other fields. The sixth man had become bored with his work, despite his success and the financial rewards he had received.

The leisure activities of four of the men were primarily family-centered. The other two men, although involved in such family-centered activities, appeared to receive major gratification from leisure activities with male friends.

All of the men described themselves as conscientious, hard-driving, aggressive, and, at the same time, very much involved with others and obtaining gratification from interpersonal relationships at work, in the family, and in leisure activities. The physical health of all six was excellent.

These men related with directness and spontaneity. They were perceived by members of the research team as open and genuine without evidence of defensiveness.

The five fathers in the working-class black families had, of course, very different work experiences. Four of the men were employed in semi-skilled jobs and one was disabled from an automobile accident. Two of the employed men had worked for their current employer for many years, and a third man was involved with his father in their own construction and house repair company. The other employed man had a series of semi-skilled jobs and had worked for his current employer only a few months. None of the men had supervisory responsibilities, and three were paid by the hour. Although the self-employed builder had no regrets about his vocational choice, the other three men expressed varying degrees of regret about their failure to have obtained a college education and, consequently, a better job. Although several of the men claimed to "like" their jobs, when pressed for *what* they liked about their work, each responded that he liked the people he worked with. They had little enthusiasm about the work itself.

Two of the men had turned to religion following a severe life crisis: one an accident and disability that precluded physical work; the other, conviction and a brief prison sentence for embezzlement. Both of these men described being seriously depressed following these events. In both instances the depression disappeared following a "calling" to preach, and they have been involved in part-time preaching activities for several years, which brought them much obvious satisfaction.

The leisure activities of all five of the men were primarily family-centered, although a few occasionally played pool and had a few beers with friends.

Four of the five fathers in this sample described "wild" periods in young adulthood characterized by drinking, womanizing, and vocational instability. All four of these men currently have patterns of stable family life and work experience which they ascribe to some combination of religion and marriage. They seemed happy and expressed clearly a sense of good fortune for the ways in which their lives had turned out.

Although two of the men had hypertension and another was disabled from an accident, they all lived active lives and their diseases and disabilities seemed not to interfere with day-to-day pursuits. Four of the five men were evaluated at average or better levels of current psychological adustment.

Mothers

The mothers in both socioeconomic groups of families clearly expressed their convictions that the family was the primary source of their
personal satisfaction. In the more affluent group, four of the six women
had extensive activities outside the family—civic work, involvement
in social clubs, and a large circle of friends. Often these women left
their homes after their husbands had gone to work and the children
to school and the house had been "straightened," returning before the
children came home from school. Despite the pleasure this level of activity brought them, the core of their self-concept was their roles as
wives and mothers.

The mother who was employed as a full-time professional preferred her work to keeping the house, but her obvious commitment to
her profession did not seem to detract from the pleasure she received
from the roles of wife and mother.

The sixth mother was not involved in outside activities and spent
most of each day about the home. Although she valued her family very
much, there was an element of mild to moderate, chronic dissatisfaction in her presentation. She was the only woman from this sample
to share some reservations about having had "too many children."

All six of these women were actively involved in planning and providing leadership to family-centered leisure activities. In addition, however, five of the six women derived obvious pleasure from adult leisure
activities involving their husbands and other couples. Going out to dinner, having friends to the house, a movie or the theater were all part
of their week-to-week living. All six women were in good physical
health, and five of the six were evaluated as functioning at above average levels of psychological adaptation.

The lives of the five mothers from the working-class black families
were very different. Three of them had full-time jobs. The two women
employed as domestic servants did not like their jobs and their working was clearly a matter of necessity. The one mother employed in a
skilled job also had to work because of her husband's disability. She
enjoyed her work, however, and looked forward to it each day. These
three working mothers had what appeared to be the most difficult life
circumstances of any of the parents in either sample. In addition to
their work, they had the major responsibility for the home and childcare

and, although their husbands and older children offered some assistance, their burden was heavy, and they went to bed very tired most evenings.

The family was the heart of these five women's lives. They were proud of their children and looked back at severe economic struggles early in their marriages with a sense of accomplishment. Despite having no economic reserves and a family income that barely covered the necessities, they judged their current circumstances to be much better than those during earlier years, and they took pride in what they had accomplished.

Most of their leisure time was involved in church activities. For these women, religion and the family formed the matrix of their lives. Church attendance was routine, and positions of leadership in church activities common. They also participated in child-related organizations such as the PTA or Scouting. Two common findings in the individual interviews of these five women were the importance of the extended family and the satisfaction of helping others.

All the women were genuine, warm, and direct with members of the research team. There often was a poignant eloquence in their descriptions of themselves, their families, and their lives.

The Marital Relationships

The marital relationship is understood as a construct that transcends the personalities of the two spouses. Marriages have emergent qualities that reflect the complementarity of the relationship for the spouses.

We have found it useful to assess marital relationships from two major perspectives: power and intimacy. In both samples of families the parents shared power. Each parent appeared to admire and respect his or her spouse's strengths. Together they formed a team which provided strong leadership to the family, with neither the intense parental competitiveness nor the skewed dominant/submissive distribution of power that are observed so commonly in families of lesser competence.

Differences were apparent, however, in regard to the level of intimacy in these marriages. As we use the term, *intimacy* refers to a level of communication within a relationship that enables two persons to share with each other their inner thoughts, feelings, fears, and dreams about which they feel a sense of vulnerability.

The individual interviews of the parents in the more affluent sample demonstrated that this aspect of the marital relationship was present and very important in four of the six couples. Each spouse emphasized its specialness: "I've never been able to talk to anyone like I can him (her) — it's a very special kind of thing." For couples who have this trusting openness, the marital relationship is experienced as the strongly cathected core of the individual's life. Such couples have a life that is separate from their strong investment in their children. In such families the parental relationship is the strongest, most affectively charged coalition in the family.

None of the five couples in the working-class families described this type of marital relationship. Although there was obvious affection and much respect for each other, this level of communication was not present. "He's good at listening and when I'm upset he'll take the time to hear me out," one wife reported — but it was obvious that there was much she did not feel free to talk about. This was typical for these five couples and represents a distinct difference in the two samples.

A second difference was that fewer of the spouses in the working-class families reported high levels of satisfaction in their sexual relationships. The couples from the more affluent families reported variable frequencies of sexual intercourse (from one or two times per month to four to five times per week), but regardless of frequency each spouse reported high levels of satisfaction. The couples from the working-class families reported an average frequency of one to two times per week, but with three of the couples the wife knew that the husband preferred a higher frequency. Although these husbands seemed to understand their wives' lack of enthusiasm, once or twice a week did not entirely meet the husband's sexual needs. The wives' major complaint was that they were often "too tired." Although this phrase may often be used an as excuse for other sources of absent interest, it had a valid ring for these often burdened women.

The Adolescent Children

The adolescents in these two groups of families share family environments that are remarkably similar, but experience socioeconomic environments that are markedly different. It is important, therefore, to compare how they are alike and how they differ. These similarities and differences may be understood from the following descriptive categories from the individual exploratory interviews.

Personal Relationship Skills. Individuals in both groups of adolescents were friendly, open, and easygoing toward the interviewer. In both groups, the young people appeared to be secure in their sense of self. This self-confidence was particularly impressive in the black adolescents because several had never had a comparable interview with a white adult.

Ability to Describe Self. Teenagers in both of these groups demonstrated some ability to describe themselves in terms of complex needs, drives, aspirations, and motivations. There was some difference, however, between the two groups. The black adolescents were less likely to describe themselves in terms as three-dimensional as were the white teenagers. In particular, the white teenagers seemed to be gaining mastery of understanding the difference between their own desires and societal and parental expectations. The black adolescents seemed to have greater difficulty in separating their desires from parental expectations.

Active/Passive Orientation. Individuals in both groups were active, assertive youngsters. They were "doers" who were involved in a wide variety of activities.

Educational Achievements and Aspirations. Individuals in both these groups were good students, with above average grades. Honor roll performance was common. There was, however, a subtle difference with regard to attitudes toward attending school. The black youngsters thought of education as the pathway out of lower-income occupations. These youngsters often utilized the most advanced programs the public school system had to offer. For example, a majority of them were either in honors programs or attending magnet schools (high schools with specialized curricula for various vocations). They were proud of their schools. One youngster talked about his almost all black high school:

"It's a great school if you want to learn. . . . All of the other schools, they're usually down on Green, but after they transfer and come over there, then they see how it really is. And most people . . . well, we had the Governor come over once and he couldn't believe it was Green—you know, no people in the halls and no paper in the halls, no writing on the walls, around the school was clean, and the wind didn't pick up and blow trash around. Other than that, they were shocked to know this was really Green and we're striving to come up from the bottom."

Of his aspiration in life, another young black male said:

"Ten years? I will be . . . let's see . . . I plan to be living in Dallas . . . I don't know if I will be married or not. I haven't thought about that. But, I plan to have a good job. I plan to be somebody . . . worth something—popular . . . that's what I want to be. *Somebody*."

This adolescent went on to relate his goals to the need to use the school system to achieve them.

The white adolescents, while being good students, seemed to take for granted that they were headed for college. Often they expressed some degree of boredom about school or uncertainty that education was necessarily the path to their aspired goals.

Extracurricular Activities. Adolescents in both of these groups were involved in a variety of extracurricular activities. They served on student councils, as presidents and members of clubs, in honor societies, and on athletic teams. There was little difference between the groups in the level of extracurricular activities. One minor difference was that the black girls participated more in athletic activities than did their white agemates.

Work. There was a marked difference in the amount of compensated employment done by youngsters in these two groups. The white adolescents had tasks around the house; the black adolescents performed fewer of these kinds of chores, but almost all had parttime jobs.

Future Orientation. Youngsters in both groups were oriented toward the future, and their plans seemed reasonable in terms of their abilities and ambitions. The white adolescents assumed that the future would work out well because the past had. The black adolescents, on the other hand, did not assume that a successful future would come as a matter of course. Rather consistently they articulated a combination of attributes that would lead to successful futures: honesty, hard work, the ability to get along with people, education, and achievement. Adolescents in both groups aspired to join the ranks of people in respected occupations. Many of the white adolescents wanted to be doctors, lawyers, or scientists. Most of the youngsters in the black group, however, aspired to better paid work than that of their parents, but not necessarily in the professional ranks.

Social Relationships. Adolescents in both of these groups had wide circles of acquaintances. Apparently these teenagers were respected by, and popular with, their peers. In both groups, the importance of one or two close, same-sex friends was stated. One subtle difference was that the black adolescents made statements suggesting they were particular in defining their close friends because most of the young people in their social and educational milieu were not headed toward the same succcess to which they aspired.

Heterosexual Relationships. In the area of heterosexual relationships, there was a major difference. Youngsters in the white group expressed serious interest in the opposite sex at about the time they were allowed to drive a car (age 16). The black adolescents' heterosexual interests began earlier, for both boys and girls. Almost half had had intercourse with more than one partner at the time of the interview. Those who had not, however, discussed intense peer pressure to experience it. Although most of the white adolescents had had "going steady" relationships, none reported having had intercourse.

Attitude Toward Parents. Adolescents in both groups expressed positive feelings toward both parents. In both groups there was a slight inclination to view the mother as the parent with whom they could more easily discuss sensitive topics. In both groups the father was more likely to be seen as the disciplinarian.

Youngsters in both groups saw their parents as stricter than the parents of their peers. Although they complained occasionally about this strictness, they also felt that rules and discipline were fair and that it was a source of their own and their family's strength. One of the white youngsters stated:

"Well, I'm glad that they are strict because some of the people I know who don't have strict parents do bad things and get into lots of trouble."

Problems with Authority, Legal Problems, Substance Usage. None of the youngsters in either sample had any significant conflicts with authority.

The major hypothesis that this research project was designed to test was that the most competent working-class black families would be shown to have a basic family organizational structure that was rigid and characterized by one dominant parent, usually the mother. The dominant parent would be seen to be the core of the family's strength, and the more submissive parent would be seen as making little contribution to leadership in the family. Our results do not confirm the major hypothesis. The most competent working-class black families are much more like than different from the most competent middle- and upper-middle-class white families studied 12 years earlier. The parents share power and together provide effective leadership for the family.

CHAPTER 7

Some Interpretations
of the Findings

THE DIFFERENCES IN FAMILY COMPETENCE

In earlier chapters we described the Continuum of Family Competence and the values upon which this approach to family nosology is based. Raters, one black and two white, blind to other data, agreed significantly in the Global Health/Pathology ratings assigned to each family in this sample. The families were assigned ratings that varied from "optimal" or most competent to "dysfunctional" or least competent. Differences in family competence were illustrated both by contrasting the five families rated as most competent with the five families rated as least competent and by presenting detailed accounts of families representative of both groups.

The ratings of family competence are based on the use of scales designed to measure crucial aspects of family interaction. It is no surprise, therefore, that there are striking differences in the interactional processes that characterize the two extreme groups. The most competent families are characterized by relationship processes that, in theory, not only facilitate autonomy, but also provide support and encourage maturation. The least competent families demonstrate relationship processes that neither facilitate autonomy nor provide support or encourage maturation. As a consequence, we expected and found that, on the average, members of the two groups of families demonstrated different levels of psychological health.

Although we did not specifically predict that the most competent families would be more involved with the surrounding community, that finding is in keeping with the systems theory postulate that well-functioning family systems have higher levels of interchange with their contexts than do less well-functioning family systems.

The finding that the fathers in the least competent families had serious chronic diseases was not predicted and may reflect the reciprocal relationship between family interaction and physical health status. Family interactions have been shown to influence individual vulnerability to disease, and disease, particularly if severe and chronic, to influence what goes on in the family.

The prediction that the most competent working-class families would demonstrate a dominant-submissive structure and the interactional processes associated with that structure was not fulfilled. The most competent working-class families were much like the most competent more affluent families. Within this sample of working-class families, however, there was a significant difference between the income levels of the most and least competent families. Although this finding must be viewed with caution because of the small sample size, it supports the hypothesis of a critical threshold of income below which it is increasingly difficult to maintain a family structure characterized by shared parental leadership and the other relationship processes that characterize competent families. As family income approaches and dips below the poverty level, the major task of the family becomes physical survival. The most adaptive family structure under those circumstances may be dominant-submissive. If this structure fails to deal with the threat, the family may move to a structure characterized by constant conflict and, ultimately, disorganization and disintegration of the family. The Bradley family in Chapter 5 illustrates what appears to be a failing dominant-submissive structure where the stress of a serious disease in a family member is added to their economic stress.

Several qualifications are required. We do not suggest that all families undergo structural change when facing severe economic stress; rather, that there is an increased probability of such an occurrence. Stresses other than economic ones may also induce a move toward family structural rigidity and, ultimately, disintegration, as Anthony's work with families facing a potentially fatal disease in a family member attests.[1]

A second caveat is that a number of factors play important roles in whether or not a particular family undergoes structural change. These factors may include the individual strengths and liabilities of family members' personalities, the presence of a supportive extended family and other support groups, the cohesiveness of the surrounding community, and the effectiveness of helping agencies.

A third caveat is that the hypothesis may oversimplify matters that are extremely complex. For example, the conceptualization attends only to the family as responsive to the socioeconomic context and does not consider the impact of family competence on the family's socioeconomic status, a variant of what has been called the "drift" hypothesis for individuals. Longitudinal family studies will be required to illuminate these complex, and often circular, relationships.

Although there is a vast sociologic literature regarding the disorganizing impact of socioeconomic factors on the family, the studies have such a macroscopic focus that they have limited use in either supporting or questioning our hypothesis. An example of this type of focus involves defining a stable family as one in which both spouses are present in the home. Although this allows many useful comparisons with other types of families, it does not (and is not meant to) describe variations within such "stable" families. It is precisely such variations with which our hypothesis is concerned.

Elder has reported longitudinal data that have implications for this hypothesis.[2] Using two well-known longitudinal cohorts, he explores the impact of the Great Depression on family patterns, adolescent personality, and adult experience. For our purposes, the following is relevant: Young male children in families that experienced serious economic deprivation were shown to be less well-adjusted during adolescence than a control group whose families did not experience such economic stress. If, however, the parental relationship (as evaluated before the economic deprivation) had a strong affectionate bond and mutual understanding, the adverse influence on male children noted in adolescence did not occur. Elder reported that if such a strong parental relationship did not preexist, the job loss of the father was associated with a growing "emotional centrality and power of the mother" and a more estranged and peripheral status of the father, and the father-son relationship suffered, with adverse consequences for the youngster during later adolescent years.

From the viewpoint of our hypothesis, it seems clear that Elder is describing a family pattern similar to that which we have called "dominant-submissive" and that this pattern may evolve under socioeconomic stress.

Other differences between the most and least competent working-class families require elaboration. These include the age and educational status of the parents, family size, the results of intelligence testing, the religious beliefs and practices of the two groups, and the differing family value orientations.

The parents in the least competent families were older, had more children, and had less schooling than the parents from the most competent families. More of them grew up in rural areas, and more of the fathers described their childhoods as both economically and emotionally deprived. Although the small sample size makes interpretation hazardous, we believe that these findings lend themselves to a hypothesis to be tested with a larger sample. This hypothesis involves the impact of unfavorable early life circumstances in family of origin, both economic and emotional, on the competence of the adult-life family of creation. Fathers who grew up under conditions of extreme deprivation are more likely to drop out of school early, go to work in low paying jobs, marry several times, have many children, and, as spouses and parents, participate in the evolution of rigid, dominant-submissive families. In such families, these fathers were more likely to be the dominant spouse, although some "selected" a dominant wife and, within the family, played the more passive and submissive role.

The major and related themes in dominant-submissive families are two: the need to control (oneself and others) and the need to avoid intimacy. Within such families, life is lived as if close relationships are dangerous. The parents in these families, particularly the fathers, seem unable to undo the effects of severe childhood deprivation.

We know that some of the parents from the most competent families, both in this study and in our earlier one, described comparable childhood deprivation, yet they have been able to participate as spouses and parents in the evolution of families that do not need to control others nor avoid intimacy. On the other hand, clinicians often see individuals with severe deprivation in early life who never marry and remain distant loners all their lives. How can we understand the attempts of the parents in the least competent families to have families, to live lives of interpersonal connectedness, however controlled and distant? To understand better will require studying both families and individuals over time. Longitudinal studies in which the development of the family is an important perspective are sorely needed.

There are differences in the results of intelligence testing between the individuals comprising this sample of families and those comprising the white middle- and upper-middle-class families studied earlier. Although the literature is complex, measured intelligence is influenced by both socioeconomic status and ethnicity. Individuals in lower socioeconomic groups, on the average, score less well on standard intellectual tests than do individuals from higher socioeconomic groups. Members of ethnic minorities, on the average, score less well than do members of the white majority. Loehlin, Lindzey, and Spuhler, for example, estimate that these two factors predict 36% of the variance in children's intellectual achievement.[3] They note, however, that the variance predictable from ethnic membership could be predicted instead by other variables associated with ethnic membership, including socioeconomic status and family structure.

What needs emphasis is the tremendous variation in measured intelligence within any social class or ethnic group. Such variation was reflected in this sample of black working-class families. The differences in measured intelligence in the members of the most and least competent families may reflect the lower socioeconomic status of the least competent families. That such is not the complete answer, however, is suggested by the following: If the three families with incomes below the poverty levels are excluded and replaced in the analysis by three families ranked next lowest in family competence, the income differences between the most and least competent families are obliterated (top five families, $12,884, and bottom five families $12,440). However, significant differences in measured intelligence persist (top five families, N of 23, IQ = 96.78; bottom five families, N of 20, IQ = 75.1). Although the numbers are small, the data suggest that family competence and measured intelligence are correlated. (The difference of means test provides a t of 4.67 with 32 degrees of freedom, $p < .0005$.) We would assume that such an effect is reciprocal or circular, in that family competence influences measured intelligence, which, in turn, influences family competence. We did not find these differences in measured intelligence, however, in the most and least competent more affluent white families in the earlier study. This suggests that the apparent relationship between family competence and measured intelligence may operate only in lower socioeconomic groups, ethnic minorities, or below a certain threshold of measured intelligence, at least when intelligence is measured by tests standardized primarily on white middle-class samples.

Group differences in measured intelligence between black and white samples have been the subject of much debate. Three major perspectives have been articulated. The first involves the unsuitability of intelligence tests for those who do not live within the mainstream of middle-class white America. This point of view essentially dismisses the group differences in measured intelligence as reflecting an inappropriate choice of instruments.

A second perspective accepts the validity of the test differences and interprets the lower group average scores of members of ethnic minorities as a reflection of deprivation — primarily socioeconomic, but also quality of education and the low value placed on books and reading. A third perspective accepts the differences and theorizes about a genetic basis. This most controversial perspective provokes much conflict, and the presumably scientific data upon which it is based have been severely assailed as, for example, by Piel.[4]

Our thinking about this issue has been influenced by individuals in this sample like Mr. and Mrs. Hooper, whose statements are quoted in Chapters 1 and 5. Despite their low scores on vocabulary and abstraction testing, their statements are seen to reflect a level of thoughtful expressiveness which is not measured by the Shipley-Hartford or other standardized tests.

A striking difference between the most and least competent families is the role that religion plays in family life. How much of this finding reflects the small sample size and the fact that one-third of the families were referred to the project by the ministerial alliance is impossible to know, but the differences are clear-cut. Religious beliefs and activities were at the core of family life for the most competent families and appeared less important to the least competent families. Parents and children from the most competent families attended church with greater frequency, more often prayed together, and clearly used Biblical concepts as orienting cognitive structures around which life is viewed and lived. There was greater variation in this regard among members of least competent families, but as a group they were less involved in religious activities and did not use Biblical concepts as orienting life structures.

These differences in the role of religion were not present in the most and least competent families in the earlier studied sample of more affluent whites. It is important to emphasize, however, that those data were collected in the late 1960s and early 1970s. There is evidence of a growing involvement in religion in this country. A recent survey, for example, revealed that three out of four persons consider themselves religious.[5] The data from this survey suggest that a person's religious values — or lack of them — are a more accurate prediction of behavior than are race, sex, age, income, education, occupation, or political persuasion. The data from this sample suggesting that better functioning families are more involved with religion do not, however, explain the nature of the interrelationship between family competence and religious beliefs and activities. This relationship is complex, and explanations which only emphasize the role that religious beliefs and activities play in facilitating family competence, or that family competence plays in facilitating religious beliefs and activities, in all probability are simplistic. Longitudinal family studies are needed to illuminate the complex interactions between family religious orientation and family competence.

Salvation is ranked as the most important value by the members of the most competent families and the least important value by members of the least competent families. This, of course, is the most profound difference possible in the use of the Rokeach Value Survey and underscores the relationship between family competence and religious beliefs and activities in this sample. There are other differences, however, in the value orientations of members of these two groups of families. Family security and happiness are highly ranked by both groups:

The most competent families rank wisdom and self-respect higher than do the members of the least competent families. The latter rank a comfortable life, a world of peace, and an exciting life higher than do members of more competent families. These differences can be interpreted in a number of ways, but it is possible that the pain and conflict within the least competent families influence family members to value highly comfort, peace, and happiness. Contrary to romantic speculations, family conflict, if chronic and seemingly unresolvable, is not exciting — but repetitious, dull, and wearing. That members of families in which such conflict is omnipresent should value highly an exciting life is, perhaps, no surprise. Such reasoning, however, presumes that the level of family competence influences value orientations and does not consider the ways that the values brought to the family by the parents may influence, positively or negatively, the development of family competence. Longitudinal family studies are obviously needed in this area also.

The differences noted in the terminal values are absent when the two groups of families' instrumental values are studied. Loving, self-controlled, forgiving, and clean are descriptors ranked highly by both groups. The most competent families rank honesty in their top five values, whereas the least competent families rank ambitious in their top five. The findings suggest that these two groups of families differ significantly in *what* they value but do not differ in the processes through which they wish those values to be achieved.

Similarities and Differences in Most Competent Families

In Chapter 6 we described the many ways in which the most competent working-class black families and the most competent middle- and upper-middle-class white families are alike and the few ways in which they appear to differ. Our data are consistent with the findings of several other observers. The Newsons, for example, studied 700 families in England.[6] They used individual interviews with the mothers, and their report is particularly useful with regard to social class differences in parenting. They report data that confirm the impression of social scientists that there has been a shift over the last few generations from largely authoritarian toward largely democratic modes of childrearing. As the social scale is descended, however, more parents cling to the authoritarian mode of parenting. Although they acknowledge that their interpretation of this finding is not fashionable, they suggest it is a reflection of the "traditions, belief systems, and techniques of child socialization which are functionally related to the sorts of lives which their members lead, and to their expectations about the adult roles in society which their children will ultimately play" (p. 141).

The Newsons emphasize that authoritarian patterns of childrearing are found more frequently in the families of unskilled workers and that many features of such families are shared by the economically underprivileged in urban communities around the world and in societies that are very different from our own. They also note that, "it [authoritarianism] has probably evolved in such a way that it allows parents and their children at least to survive and cope at a certain level . . . " (p. 144).

For the majority of the Newsons' working-class families, however, the structure of the family has become more egalitarian and democratic. Despite this change, they found that the children in middle-class families, in contrast to working-class children, are future-oriented, more sheltered and protected, are expected to learn more communication skills, and, as young children, are less exposed to physical punishment. The most competent working-class families in our study, like their more affluent across-the-city counterparts, were more democratic. Their adolescent children were future-oriented and had considerable communication skills. They were not, however, as sheltered and protected as their middle-class white agemates. We do not have data on physical punishment during earlier childhood.

Henggeler and Tavormina have also published data that suggest social class and ethnic differences in family interaction have been exaggerated by uncontrolled sampling and other methodological factors.[7] They indicate that earlier researchers described lower-class families as less warm and more conflicted than middle-class families. Other investigators have reported the same differences (less warmth and greater conflict) between black and white families. Henggeler and Tavormina point out that these differences have most often been interpreted as psychosocial deficits in lower-class families and in black families. They present data from their own unusually well-controlled interactional study of intact, "well-adjusted" lower- and middle-class black and white family triads. Family competence in this study was defined but not directly measured. The defining criteria were intactness, no history of psychiatric referral or felony conviction, and referred as "well-adjusted" by an agency or professional. Our work indicates that the use of such criteria results in families representing a broad range of measured family competence.

Although there were self-reported differences between their four groups of families in the areas of affect, conflict, and dominance, these differences were not confirmed by direct rating of family interactions. Direct rating yielded few race and class differences. One difference, similar to a finding in our study to be discussed in a subsequent section, was that of less warmth and affection in the marital dyads in the working-class families as contrasted to the middle-class families. The authors caution, however, that these qualitative findings could be contaminated by differences in verbal IQs, family size, or rater bias.

Based on their assumption that all the families were at equal levels of competence, Henggeler and Tavormina indicate that it is invalid to assume that there is but one group of family characteristics associated with family competence. This is an unusually well designed study and its findings parallel many of our own — particularly in the finding that there are few differences across social class and ethnic groups. We believe, however, that the differences in interpretations result from the differences between Henggeler and Tavormina's assumptions of equal levels of competence and our use of a direct rating of family competence.

These two studies are interpreted to support our finding that the similarities between this sample of working-class black families and the previously studied more affluent white families far outweigh the differences. The differences we have noted were in family style rather than the family interactional processes.

A major difference involved the absence of evidence of marital intimacy in the black working-class families. Although the spouses shared power, they did not describe a reciprocal sharing of vulnerabilities. This type of trusting openness was so obviously a central feature of the parental relationship in the most competent more affluent white families that its absence in this sample was striking. Clearly, the spouses in the working-class families respected each other, were proud of their children, and had a strong affectionate bond. They did not, however, demonstrate or report high levels of intimate communication. In this way they are more like the spouses in the competent but pained families from the white sample who, in addition, manifested unequal distribution of power, often strong mother-child coalitions, an absence of spontaneity, and a general family tendency to avoid shared affect. The black working-class families did not reveal such characteristics; indeed, the lack of intimate marital communication stood nearly alone in distinguishing these families from the most competent, more affluent families.

There are numerous interpretations possible. This absence of deep levels of verbal sharing could be a reflection of the IQ differences, different types of verbal skills, ethnic differences, or other variables. We favor a hypothesis related to socioeconomic stress. These couples described difficult times earlier in their marriages, characterized by both lack of effective management skills with which to survive on a marginal income and the husband's "wildness" before settling into a stable marital pattern. Their current, strong parental coalition with relatively equal power appeared to be an accomplishment of more recent years, in contrast to the economically more fortunate couples. These more affluent couples either had better management skills or needed fewer such skills because of more favorable economic circumstances. There was also no history of early "wildness" on the part of the husbands, who seemed from the start of the marriages to have been self-disciplined and family centered. We suggest that the development of marital intimacy requires this type of context and that such a context has been present for a much longer period of time in the more affluent couples. This raises the question of whether longitudinal studies would demonstrate the later development of marital intimacy in the working-class couples. We believe the matter to be of considerable importance, particularly in light of the studies that suggest that the presence of an intimate relationship may protect stressed women of lower socioeconomic classes from the development of depressive syndromes.[8]

A second difference involves marital sexual satisfaction. The working-class couples did not report the same level of shared sexual satisfaction as the more affluent couples. The most common theme was the wife's fatigue and the husband's desire for more frequent intercourse. Although here again a number of explanations are possible, the clinicians who did the individual interviews tended to accept at face value the reports of these individuals. The wives had ample reason for fatigue and often declined to yield to their husbands' desires. Indirectly, this is another statement about shared power — their right to refuse. Mr. Hooper emphasized another way in which economic factors impinge on marital sexuality in stating, "Well, you know, a woman is not all there if she's worried about other things. A man, though, is usually ready."

When we compare the five most competent working-class families and the six most competent middle- and upper-middle-class families with regard to the role of religion in family life, we are, of course, dealing with a very small sample. The importance of religion to most of these families is impressive. This may be a sampling bias and certainly needs replication with a larger sample of highly competent families. However, it is well to emphasize also that the mental health professions, as a group, may underestimate the adaptive value of religious beliefs and activities.

The adolescents in the two groups of families were much more alike than different. With few exceptions they were well-functioning, active, energetic, and future-oriented youngsters. The more affluent adolescents took future success for granted, whereas the lower-income black adolescents clearly knew they were in a struggle. They believed the struggle was going to be won — but only through their efforts. In this effort, they rejected the attitudes and values of many of their peers, for whom the future was less important than the present. At the time of data collection strong family ties and religion were important to them in this struggle.

The working-class black adolescents had earlier involvement and were much more experienced in heterosexual activities than their more affluent white agemates. They described peer pressure, often intense, to have sexual relationships early in adolescence and, in this regard, few resisted such pressure. Family ties, values, and injunctions did not prevail. Why this is so is open to question. Almost certainly it does not reflect the operation of a single causal factor. Cultural traditions, peer pressure, easy availability of sexual partners, the need for some immediate gratification in young lives in which postponement and the future seem so important, changes in adolescent sexual mores during the years separating the two studies, and other factors may play a role.

Throughout this discussion and, indeed, the entire text we have made no effort to ascribe differences between this sample and the previously studied families to ethnic variables. The reasons for this are several. First, although our original design called for three groups of lower-income families (black, white, and Mexican-American), we were unable to find support for that study. If we had been more fortunate, the results would have allowed us to clarify ethnic differences in family structure and function in that socioeconomic class. Our hypothesis would have been (and still is) that those three groups of families would be much more alike than different — if the level of family competence is held constant. That does not mean that we anticipated no ethnic differences in family structure and function, but that such differences would be relatively slight in contrast to the similarities.

A second factor is the striking similarities found between these two groups of highly competent families which differ so vastly along socioeconomic parameters. These similarities have been so striking to us that it seemed parsimonious to consider initially the few differences as most likely a reflection of the socioeconomic differences. We recognize that it is equally valid to ascribe these differences to other factors. It is obvious that further work will have to be undertaken to sort out socioeconomic and ethnic variables. This, we believe, should not detract, however, from an appreciation of how much these highly competent black working-class families and the highly competent more affluent white families are alike.

As we have indicated at several points in this text, we did not expect to find such striking similarities. Having found them we have reported them openly, although not without concern that they will be used for other purposes. Those readers, for example, who subscribe to an "anything is possible if you work hard enough" ethic could use these findings to minimize the role of socioeconomic stress on families and opt for an even greater laissez-faire family policy than now exists in current government. We wish to emphasize our disagreement with that stance—a disagreement based on both scientific and moral grounds. We have no data on how common high levels of family competence in lower socioeconomic groups actually are, and the well-publicized data about family fragmentation and the growth of single-parent families indicate the magnitude of the social problem and the need for innovative social solutions.

From a very different perspective, those readers who subscribe to an orientation that emphasizes the value of ethnic differences may react to our finding of much sameness with disbelief and negative affect.

Another group may point out that definitions of individual psychological adaptation and family competence are but value-ladened, middle-class stereotypes of what we think "ought to be." We have tried to make our position clear: that values do underlie such concepts and that it is the task of the researcher to be open and clear about them. If some readers, for example, do not believe that the cardinal tasks of the family, after survival, are what we have articulated, they should not and doubtlessly will not pay any attention to our research findings. We believe that producing autonomous children and stabilizing parental personality are the key overarching tasks of the family, and our data demonstrate that working-class black families with certain characteristics accomplish those tasks, on the average, more effectively than do families with other characteristics.

REFERENCES

1. Anthony, J. E. The impact of mental and physical illness on family life. *American Journal of Psychiatry*, 1970, *127*. 138–146.
2. Elder, G. H. Historical change in life patterns and personality. In P. B. Baltes & L. G. Brim (Eds.), *Life span development and behavior,* Vol. 2. New York: Academic Press, 1979.
3. Loehlin, J. C., Lindzey, G., & Spuhler, J. N. Cross-group comparisons of intellectual abilities. In *Race differences in intelligence.* San Francisco: W. H. Freeman & Co., 1975, 165–175.
4. Piel, G. IQ: Failing the test. *The Sciences,* January, 1978, *18*(1).
5. Research and Forecasts, Inc. *The Conneticut Mutual Life Report on American values in the '80s: The impact of belief.* Hartford, Conneticut Mutual Life Insurance Co., 1981, p. 17.
6. Newson, J., & Newson, E. Changes in concepts of parenthood. In K. Elliott (Ed.), *The family and its future.* London: J & A Churchill, 1970.

7. Henggeler, S. W., & Tavormina, J. B. Social class and race differences in family interaction: Pathological, normative, or confounding methodological factors? *Journal of Genetic Psychology,* 1980, *137,* 211-222.

8. Brown, G. W. & Harris, T. *Social origins of depression.* New York: Free Press, 1978.

CHAPTER 8

Relationship to Other Studies

The issue of how the findings of this study relate to other accounts of black family life needs articulation. This chapter provides the reader a selected review of a large body of literature. Staples and Mirande,[1] in a recent decennial review of the literature on minority families, note that in the decade of the 1970s over 50 books and 500 articles related to black families were published. It should be recalled, however, that the intent of our research was not to expand this literature on black families in any global way but, rather, to test a specific hypothesis that the most competent families in a black working-class sample would be more rigid than the most competent families in a middle- and upper-middle-class sample. The project, therefore, was not designed specifically to illuminate that which is unique about black families, but rather to study the impact of socioeconomic stress on family structure and function. We wished to explore the utility of the concept of family competence in a cohort of families very different from those used in developing the concept.

Selection of black families as the focus of our research moved us into an arena in which there has been considerable scientific debate. We were aware that in the past black family research had been dominated by a perspective that emphasized pathology. The black family was often viewed as a dysfunctional unit, characterized by irresponsible fathers, matriarchical mothers, and pervasive disorganization. Moynihan's assessment of the status of the black family from census data, for example, emphasizes the "deterioration of the Negro society."[2] Because Moynihan was a high ranking government employee, this report achieved the status of an official government publication. It galvanized researchers to action and has led to both a broad range of empirical and nonempirical studies and a more careful appraisal of the competing ideological perspectives in black family research. Moynihan's negative stereotyping demonstrates the need for a data-based recharacterization of black family life.

RESEARCH PERSPECTIVES

A number of published reports are available that deal with important methodological issues involved in studying black families. These need to be considered carefully when relating the present study to other studies. The problems of bias are predominant concerns in these reports. An early commentator on this issue was Cedrik X.[3] He makes a strong argument for careful examination of the interpretive framework in scientific studies and the validity of the information gained from such studies. His position clearly is that the interpretive framework for analysis of black families will be faulty if based upon assumptions associated with the "reality" of white researchers.

Nobles[4] attempts to elucidate a theoretical framework for describing black families. He suggests that two factors are apparent in previous research: an orientation toward pathologizing and domination by white researchers. He proposes that black families need to be studied through a world view encompassing a "black reality," and he suggests reviewing African culture as a basis for understanding black families. To illustrate the need for this Afro-centric analysis of the black family, he quotes an African proverb, "He who cannot dance will say the drum is bad" (p. 687). He concludes by stating, "It seems clear that for too long, studies and research about black family life have been done by 'people who could not dance.' It is understandable that their conclusions have consistently resulted in a negative opinion about the drum [black family]" (p. 687).

Nobles's assertion that the capacity to understand a phenomenon is dependent upon the observer's perspective is examined by Merton,[5] who articulates the methodological problems of an insider/outsider bias. In its most rarified form, the insider/outsider doctrine maintains the principle that only insiders can understand the realities of alien groups, cultures, or societies. As an example of this position, only a black historian can understand black history; a black sociologist, black culture. Merton concludes that it is important to be aware of potential sociological myopia when studying other cultural groups, but that pushed to its extreme the doctrine that only insiders can understand a phenomenon is fallacious.

Sawyer[6] agrees that there are problems inherent in viewing psychological and sociological phenomena from the bias of one's own experience, but is concerned particularly with the problem of the black researcher who studies black populations. She suggests, for example, that a black researcher may have "withholding tendencies," may question how much of what he or she sees should be reported or even recorded. Excessive identification with the subject studied is another problem. One can infer from this work that scientific objectivity and appropriate distance are more a function of proper application of the scientific method than whether one is an insider or an outsider.

Mathis[7] postulates two competing perspectives influencing the study of black families. The first, an "American-dilemma" perspective related to the early research by Frazier,[8] assumes that black families are patterned after the dominant culture. The second perspective suggests that black family life is based in African culture and must be viewed as an entity independent of the dominant culture. He points out the former perspective has often stressed the dysfunctional nature of black families, and he traces a heritage of this perspective extending from the work of Frazier to that of Moynihan,[2] Rainwater,[9,10] Bernard,[11] Parker and Kleiner,[12] Blood and Wolfe,[13] and many others. These authors describe deviations from the norms of the dominant culture, such as marital instability, delinquency, pathological matriarchies, illegitimacy, and hedonism. Their underlying assumption is that black families have failed to assimilate into the dominant white culture. The second perspective suggests that black family life must be viewed as a continuation of African culture, and differences between black and white families should be assessed in terms of the norms of African culture, not as deviations from white American culture. Mathis reviews the work of sociological investigators (Herskovits,[14] Blassingame,[15] Billingsley,[16] Young,[17,18] Hill,[19] Nobles,[20] Turnbull[21]) which, in concert, lend support to this perspective. Mathis's comprehensive review documents the existence of two bodies of literature, each supporting one of the described perspectives. The fact that observers of the same phenomenon tend to reach conflicting conclusions supports the idea that biases enter this area of study. However, Mathis does not offer a perspective for studying black family life that would minimize bias.

Allen[22] calls upon researchers to become sensitized to inherent "object/subjective" biases in contemporary theorizing about black families, and he tries to identify theoretical frameworks for the study of black families. He states, "Theorists of the black family are still in pursuit of adequate theoretical frameworks for the study of black families." He describes three ideological perspectives that characterize this research. In addition to the cultural deviant perspective, he describes the perspectives of "cultural equivalent" and "cultural variant." The cultural equivalent ideology is characterized by researchers who do not attend distinctive qualities of black family life and focus only on characteristics similar to those of white families. Those researchers who, for example, place primary emphasis on social class rather than ethnic differences do black families "somewhat of an injustice by failing to acknowledge their validity as distinct cultural forms" (p. 125). Allen indicates that this perspective makes the implicit value judgment that black families constitute a legitimate focus only insofar as they approximate white middle-class families.

The cultural variant perspective views the black family as a distinct cultural form, emphasizing that distinguishing characteristics "are not necessarily taken as reflections of pathology" (p. 125). Allen quotes the work of Billingsley[16] which underscores the adaptive nature of black family differences. Although the cultural variant perspective acknowledges that family functions are more or less universal, it emphasizes the need to understand black-white family differences as responsive to contextual circumstances. Allen's helpful analysis of theoretical perspectives emphasizes the need for a combination of the cultural equivalent and cultural variant perspectives, depending upon the nature of the research questions to be answered.

Robert Staples[23] writes cogently about the problem of biases. He states, "The past history of black family research has been characterized by the reiteration of unfounded myths and stereotypes which produce in the public mind the image of black families as a pathological social unit — a system incapable of rearing individuals who can adjust to the demands of a civilized society" (p. 119). Further, he states, "Using what are presumed to be middle-class 'normal' families as measuring rods for black families has stigmatized those Afro-American families. Consequently, research on the black family is predicated on the assumption that it is a malfunctioning unit and the research problem is to assess the etiological determinants of its pathological structure. What is of concern to us is what research on the black family has produced, the reliability and validity of the research instruments used, alternative explanations of black family behavior, and questions that need to be answered in order to understand the nature and function of family life in the black community" (p. 120).

Staples reviews a number of previous studies to document his thesis. He begins by dichotomizing studies into those that generate what he calls macro-sociological theories and micro-sociological theories. A seminal example of a macro-sociological study would be that of the late black sociologist, E. Franklin Frazier.[8] Staples judges that Frazier's global and nonrigorous survey of groups of black people led to his theory that there is a state of disorganization in family life resulting from past abuses of the black family during slavery days, rapid urbanization, and economic deprivation. Staples reviews Moynihan's work[2] as a progression of macro-sociological studies leading to an erroneous theory about black family life. Staples questions Moynihan's attempt to confirm Frazier's ideas by using census data, which he interprets as showing high dissolution of black marriages, high rates of illegitimate births, high prevalence of female-headed households, and high welfare dependency. Staples states that Moynihan's biased study can be rejected if its poor methodology is assessed. Staples also reviews the macro-sociological works of Rainwater[24] and Billingsley[16] and finds problems with bias and nonrigorous methods that lead to a more pathologized picture of black families than is warranted.

Micro-sociological research deals with more focused aspects of black family life. Staples reviews the methods and findings of studies assessing such issues as dyadic relationships, sexual behavior, matriarchy, parental roles, and socialization of children. These studies vary wide-ly in the quality of assessment methods and the validity of conclusions, but overall both macro- and micro-sociological studies have diminished value because of " . . . the weak methodology employed; the superficial analysis that ensues from the use of poor research designs; biased and low samples; and inadequate research designs" (p. 133). He stresses the need for assessment of dynamic processes within the black fami-lies and concludes, ". . . past research on the black family has focused on its structural features, not its interactional processes" (p. 133). He advocates a viable sociology of black family life based not on preconceived norms of white, middle-class family structure, but upon an assessment of the actual dynamic processes occurring within black families: ". . . we must ascertain the norms and values that animate the processes of family interaction and how that process is related to the forces that have shaped it and its various expressions in American life" (p. 135).

Bagarozzi[25] notes that few investigations are available that offer in-sights into the actual internal dynamics of black families. He suggests using a systems theory paradigm as a way of transcending ethnic, ra-cial, and socioeconomic boundaries, and he reviews a number of pri-mary concepts of systems theory as they relate to a clinical under-standing of black middle-class families. Bagarozzi presents family systems theory concepts as a way of enhancing a clinician's ability to carry out family therapy with middle-class black families. Although not a research study defining and measuring system variables, his ap-proach can be related to theoretical constructs now widely used to un-derstand families of other ethnic and socioeconomic groups (Haley,[26,27] Jackson,[28] Lewis et al.[29]), and it has the potential to transcend the types of biases reviewed above.

After reviewing these contributions, which outline problems in clari-fying perspectives in studying black families, it is up to the reader to decide if the present pilot research study emerges with a fresh focus or is marred by the kind of biases described above or by others. Our own appraisal encourages us and does so for a number of reasons:

1) Our study was not stimulated by a desire to engage one side or the other of the controversy about whether black families are more pathological than, better than, or just different from white families.

2) Whereas we agree with Merton[5] that, pushed to its extreme, the doctrine that only insiders can understand a phenomenon is fallacious, we did enter the study with the idea that it was important to have black research team members involved in the process of establishing alliances and gathering and analyzing data.

3) Our work is not an attempt to achieve a global description of black families but, rather, is a focus on specific hypotheses across ethnic and socioeconomic groups using the same method of study in both groups.

4) The work uses quantifiable variables derived from family systems theory and, therefore, assesses dynamic processes within families rather than assessing them only by their own subjective descriptions. Our method, therefore, is based upon the systems theory concept called for by Bagarozzi, and moves toward the systematic assessment of the process of family interaction called for by Staples.

The reader may ask if our study can fit into one of the perspectives described in these previously published works. Within Staples' dichotomization of macro-sociological and micro-sociological, it would be a micro-sociological study. It is difficult to know how to characterize the study in terms of its confluence or deviance from an Afro-centric view of black families. One reason for this difficulty is the problem we have in conceptualizing Afro-centricity in terms that can be related to modern-day, urban black families.

Allen's analysis of theoretical perspectives emphasizes the need to combine the cultural equivalent and cultural variant perspectives in ways that reflect the nature of the research questions to be answered. We see our research project as having elements of both of these perspectives. The introduction of the concept of family competence is a crucial issue. The question is whether it is reasonable and fair to use the same yardstick to evaluate families with different socioeconomic contexts. We have done so and, contrary to our major hypothesis, found that black working-class families are very much more like than different from the more affluent white families. This finding underscores the strengths of these working-class families. Despite difficult socioeconomic circumstances, they have evolved interactional patterns that are associated with high levels of individual psychological health. Whether the few differences in these two samples of families are a reflection of the vastly different socioeconomic context, as we suspect, or represent ethnically determined patterns cannot be answered without the inclusion of working-class families from other ethnic groups in subsequent research. However, our data support the concept that basically similar standards can be used in attempting to understand the characteristics that are associated with more competent families in widely different socioeconomic contexts. Those social observers who emphasize the *inevitable* consequences of socioeconomic differences or the pathology or uniqueness of black family life will find little support in this study of a particular sample of intact, working-class black families.

TWO RECURRING AND IMPORTANT CONCEPTS

In reviewing the literature on black families, two general concepts appear in the work of various authors which are of particular relevance. These concepts are:

1) Black families are heterogeneous in structure and function.
2) Competent families can be found, and some consistent characteristics of these stronger families have been outlined.

The concept of heterogeneity is important in avoiding stereotyping of black families. There is no single type of structure characteristic of the black family. There is also tremendous variation in how black families cope with the stresses of their lives, just as there is with families of other ethnic groups (Willie,[30] Staples and Mirande,[1] Hill[19]). This concept is consistent with the finding of a continuum of family competence in white families. Another aspect of heterogeneity is the finding by some authors that how much money a family has to live on affects that family as much as the race of the family. Middle-class black families may be more similar in function to middle-class white families than to black families much lower on the socioeconomic hierarchy (Willie,[30] Staples and Mirande,[1] Heiss[31]).

Hill[19] is spokesman for the view that the turbulent history and deprivations of blacks in this country have led to the development of particular strengths and resiliencies, among which are:

1) Role adaptability by family members.
2) Strong kinship bonds.
3) Strong work orientation.
4) Strong religious orientation.
5) Strong achievement orientation.

These five characteristics have been necessary, in his opinion, for the survival, advancement, and stability of black families. Hill's assessment of these characteristics comes from survey and census data and needs to be confirmed in rigorous and more indepth studies. If we are to offer help to dysfunctional families in a rational manner, we need to know the ideal toward which we work. In Hill's words, "If, as most scholars agree, there is a need to strengthen black families, then a first-order priority should be the identification of presently existing strengths, resources, and potentials. Systematic examination of the strengths of black families should facilitate the development of national policies and programs which enhance and use these assets to their fullest potential" (p. 2).

Willie and Weinandy[32] focus on the structure and composition of families that remain stable in a very low income housing project (black and other ethnic groups). In contrasting these families to "problem families" in the same environment, they found certain characteristics to define the former group, including:

1) Significantly more of the stable families have two parents available to the children.
2) The parents in stable families had been married significantly longer.
3) Parents in the stable families were older.
4) The parents in stable families married later in life.
5) Parents in stable families were able to limit the number of children.

Our study was restricted to families with two parents in the household; yet within this group those families achieving higher ratings of family competence do not reflect the trends in Willie and Weinandy's "stable families." Their study focuses mostly on family composition and does not address the differences in processes or functioning between these two groups. In addition, it is difficult from their data to separate the issues of race and poverty. Another interpretive difficulty is the "circularity" of the study. Older, longer-married parents able to limit their family size might be expected to achieve greater marital stability. Despite these difficulties, the focus on defining competence by rigorous methods is rare in this body of literature.

The work of McQueen is another example of an attempt to assess determinants of competence.[33] He assesses 57 impoverished black families and determines that 34 of these ". . . ranked high on measures of family well-being, that is, those who were able to take care of basic family needs and realize important family values" (p. 15). He describes these as "effective copers" or "future oriented," and contrasts them with 23 ineffective families. He found that the better functioning families are more likely to be intact with a male head of the household and to have fewer children. In addition, he found certain orientations and strategies in the coping families:

1) Strong family orientation. The goals of individuals within these families were overwhelmingly family-related goals.
2) Mobility aspirations. Although the parents had no strong aspirations for improvement in their own social status, they did have such aspirations for their children, particularly their sons.
3) Quest for respectability. This was most often apparent through strong church affiliation.
4) Planning for the future in realistic economic terms.
5) Strong self-reliance during times of severe economic deprivation rather than borrowing from relatives or friends.

McQueen's findings are derived from interview data, and the themes and strategies he describes in the coping families are similar to those that emerged from our study of the more competent families in our sample.

THE INFLUENCE OF SOCIOECONOMIC CIRCUMSTANCES

The families in our study, although of working-class, were poor, and their impoverishment needs to be related to other accounts of the effect of this stressor on family life. Willie[30,34,35,36] addresses this problem in a number of publications. His and Weinandy's study[32] comparing "problem" and "stable" families in a low income population used the housing project manager to identify families in need of immediate help. He found 54 of the 678 households in such a condition; 40 of the households were listed as stable. For both groups poor education and unemployment were a way of life. Eighty percent of the problem families and 75% of the stable families had parents who had not graduated from high school. Approximately 30% of men in all families were unemployed (35% for problem and 25% for stable). Willie's study describes the crushing stress of life at this income level. He demonstrates the same stress on family life among the poor in the Cadozo area of Washington, D.C.[37] He has studied the way in which the pain of poverty was transmitted from generation to generation[38] by the chain of events of the early need to work, poor education, low paying jobs, or unemployment. Happily, he found the hypothesis that poverty is a trap from which there is no escape to be untrue. There is some intergenerational transmission of poverty, although less than generally assumed. Upward social mobility is a more common experience in this country than is the continuation of intergenerational poverty.

In Willie's study, "The Black Family and Social Class," he stresses the concept of heterogeneity.[34] That is to say, all black families are not alike, and social class affects values and coping maneuvers more than race does. He describes families in three groups: middle-class, working-class, and the lower-class, struggling poor. The latter two are particularly pertinent to our study. He calls the working-class families "the innovative marginal" and describes a number of distinguishing characteristics.

1) A struggle for survival requiring the cooperative efforts of all family members, a "heroic effort" to prevent sliding back into poverty.
2) Pride in children and sacrifice for their welfare. Pride that the children have a strong sense of morality, are respectable, and do not get in trouble.
3) Literate parents, but of limited education.
4) Limited opportunities to do things together as a family because of multiple job responsibilities.
5) A steadiness and constancy that tend to pull the family through. They tend, for example, to stay in one place and buy their homes rather than attempting to improve their position by moving frequently and renting.

6) Egalitarian relationship between parents germinated through the necessary cooperation for survival.
7) Little time for community activities, although church is important.

Distinguishing characteristics of the lower-class, "struggling poor" are:

1) Their low income status forces them to make a number of "clever, ingenious, and sometimes foolish" arrangements to survive, arrangements such as having extended family members in the home or taking in boarders or foster children for pay.
2) Boyfriend-girlfriend relationships serve to raise children "while the participants maintain their autonomy unfettered by marital bonds."
3) Conventional moral values may be eroded by the pressure of finding ways to survive.
4) The threat of disintegration is so severe there is little margin for error.
5) Movement (partners, jobs, houses, cities) is constant.
6) Very early marriage (or equivalent) and childbearing.
7) Seeking assistance from extended family or friends.
8) Little community involvement. There is a tendency to be uninvolved in or engulfed by religion.

The income criteria Willie used to define the marginal income and low income groups — when adjusted for inflation over the time difference between his study and ours — cover the income range of our sample of families. The families in our sample did show some attributes of both his socioeconomic groups. Further, there was a tendency for our more impoverished families to demonstrate the characteristics of his "struggling poor" group.

Scanzoni also addresses the issue of how economic impoverishment affects family life.[39,40] For example, he assesses marital satisfaction in both black and white families, finding strong correlations between economic satisfaction and marital satisfaction for both ethnic groups. This finding is supported by the work of other authors. For example, Renne[41] reports that black couples are more likely than white couples to be dissatisfied with their marriages, but the degree of dissatisfaction increases with decreasing amounts of income and education. Bell[42] found that very poor black women feel that their relationship to a husband is very low on the list of potential sources of satisfaction.

Galligan and Bahr[43] assessed marital stability as perceived by 1,349 married black and white women and found instability was greater for the black women than for the white, but the instability was highest in the couples with the lowest level of economic assets and education. Blood and Wolfe[44] compared marital satisfaction in "blue collar" black and white marriages and found the modal white wife in the sample was highly satisfied with her marriage, whereas the typical black wife was only moderately satisfied. What emerges when these studies are assessed in combination is the finding that being both black and poor diminishes the ability to obtain satisfaction from marriage.

DISCRIMINATION AND BLACK IDENTITY

The problems of being black, racial discrimination, and establishing an identity need to be examined as they pertain to the families in our sample. Major authors in this field, such as Willie[30] and Billingsley,[16] point out that the historical impact and the contemporary experience of racial discrimination negatively affect advancement opportunities as well as the ability to maintain a positive self-image. The subjects in our sample, when interviewed as individuals or assessed in family groups, expressed very little feeling about the impact of racial discrimination to either black or white research team members. They seemed to accept that being black meant they had an extra barrier to success because of racial discrimination, but that the barrier could be overcome, particularly by the youngsters in these families. The parents often expressed the idea that discrimination was more destructive in its historical impact, and they repeatedly told their children how much better life is than it has been when they were young. In interpreting these benign comments by our subjects, we need to keep in mind the important warning of McGee[45] that the white researcher can unknowingly use the social conditioning techniques to establish and maintain dependent and acquiescent behavior in black people.

Black self-concept is an issue central to the writing of several authors who have contributed to an understanding of black people and black families. Billingsley describes the process by which black mothers teach their children that they are different than the ethnic majority. He quotes a statement made by a mother in Jackson, Mississippi to Robert Coles:[16]

"When they asks all the questions, they ask about their color too. They more than not will see a white boy or girl and it makes them stop and think. They gets to wondering and then first thing you know, they want to know this and that about it, and I never have known what to say, except that the Lord likes everyone because he makes everyone. . . . I tell them that no matter what it's like around us, it may make us feel bad, but it's not the whole picture, because we don't make ourselves. . . . When they ask me why colored people aren't as good as whites, I tell them it's not that they're not as good; it's that they're not as rich. Then I tell them that they should separate being poor and being bad, and not get them mixed up" (p. 29).

Nobles[46] provides a critical review of other contributions to the literature on Negro self-concept. His description of the phenomenon of self-hatred by black people has received considerable attention (Adelson,[47] Radke-Yarrow and Lande,[48] Sarnoff,[49] Clark and Clark,[50] Stevenson and Stewart,[51] Radke and Trager,[52] Goodman,[53] Moreland,[54] Landreth and Johnson[55]). Clark and Clark[50] reported that the Negro does not like being a Negro. The Negro child absorbs cultural norms and learns to associate "Negro" with dirty, bad, and ugly, and "white" with clean, nice, and good. The black person, having learned the majority culture's disdain for his own race, feels disdain toward himself. Nobles, however, then reviews the work of some authors (Grossack,[56] Noel,[57] Sewad,[58] Parker and Kleiner,[59] Proshansky and Newton[60]) who demonstrated positive group identification and self-concepts ranging from mild self-satisfaction to militant black pride. In his analysis of this polarization of ideas he says, "The relationship between the orientation of most of the black self-concept research reviewed in this paper and the race of most of the researchers involved is not a statistical artifact" (p. 26). He calls for an Afro-centric reorientation of researchers to understand this issue.

We did not focus specifically on the issue of how the subjects in this project felt about themselves as black people. However, in our free-flowing discussions no statement evolved indicating either unhappiness about being black or unusual pride about it. The subjects saw themselves as people. Their identification was more with being poor (with feelings ranging from anger to resignation) and with winning the struggle to succeed in spite of it (with clearly expressed feelings of pride) than it was with being black. Billingsley[16] points out in his book how the black family's self-concept is affected by its contemporaneous interaction with multiple systems, including both the black and white society. Our families seemed to demonstrate a pragmatic ability to identify with the best qualities of each.

VALUES

The assessment of values was a major part of our research procedure, and it is of interest to review the findings of others regarding the value orientation of poor black people. Rodman[61] proposes the concept of "lower-class value stretch" as a way of understanding lower-class behavior. Poor people face a difficult contradiction in life because society is based upon both a common value system and a class-differentiated value system. In studying lower-class people in the Caribbean he found that these people stretch without abandoning the general values of society, or they develop alternate values, which helps them adjust to their deprived condition. They do not commit themselves strongly to middle-class values they cannot attain. The result is a "stretched out" value system with a low level of commitment to all the values within the range, including the culturally prevailing middle-class values.

Coyners, Farmer, and Levin[62] studied attitudes of black adolescents (predominantly very poor) in the public school system of a large Southern city and found them to rank high the following values (in order of diminishing importance): *pleasant personality, ability, friendliness, proper morals, grades in school, high ideals,* and *personal ambition.* These qualities for "getting ahead in life" have a middle-class quality and, as well, are reminiscent of the attitudes of the adolescents in our sample. The adolescents in the sample of Coyners and coworkers rated low the following charactertistics (in diminishing order of importance): *family background, good clothes, athletic ability, luck, being a white person, good looks,* and *being "slick."*

Several authors have noted the profound impact socioeconomic status has on value orientation. Yost[63] compared middle- and lower-class black families on a number of dimensions and found that middle-class blacks are ardent defenders of the society's dominant values. Willie's comparison of black families in three socioeconomic groups[34] shows that working-class black families affiliated with the culture's dominant value system and the struggling poor families pick and choose values pragmatically, which Rodman describes as "value stretch."

The instrument used in this study for assessment of values was the Rokeach Value Survey, and its developer has established norms for different ethnic and socioeconomic groups. Rokeach,[64] in reviewing the controversy engineered by the Moynihan report, suggests that if Moynihan's thesis of a self-perpetuating black subculture of poverty were correct, "then we should also expect to find the values of a 'culture of poverty' even among black Americans who are not poor or uneducated" (p. 68). In fact, the values of the more affluent and better educated differ in many ways from the values of poor, less well educated subjects. These social class differences are greater than those seen in comparing black and white Americans. In comparing 1,195 rankings by whites with 202 rankings by black individuals he found:

> Blacks and whites do not differ on religious values (salvation, forgiving) or on values that suggest hedonism or desire for immediate gratification. An exciting life and pleasure are ranked seventeenth and eighteenth down the terminal list by both white and black Americans. Self-controlled is ranked in the middle of the instrument value scale by both groups. There is no evidence here that black Americans even have the values that are supposed to be the main "stigma" of the culture of poverty (p. 68).

Of the 36 ranked values, Rokeach found the greatest difference between black and white Americans on *equality* (second for blacks and 11th for whites). The more highly ranked values by blacks are: *a comfortable life, social recognition, ambitious, clean,* and *obedient.* Ranked significantly lower by blacks are: *a sense of accomplishment, family security, mature love, national security,* and *logical, loving, and responsible.* The average black person ranks himself as being more *ambitious* than the average white person.

If socioeconomic and educational levels are controlled, the 13 significant differences between blacks and whites are reduced to 7. Rokeach suggests that this finding means that most of the differences seen between the two ethnic groups were attributable more to socioeconomic issues than to race. In fact, the only value that Rokeach found to continue to show a large undiminished difference was *equality.* The black subjects still placed a somewhat higher value on a *comfortable life* and *being clean,* and a lower value on *a world of beauty, family security,* and *loving,* although these differences were smaller than those demonstrated by comparing the two ethnic groups with matching income and educational levels. Rokeach does not clarify at which socioeconomic and educational levels these black and white subjects fall in the second comparison. It may be he did not compare poor working-class blacks (as in our sample) with white Americans of the same socioeconomic status.

In a different analysis Rokeach contrasts the poor with the wealthy (of all races). Of all values, *being clean* best separates these two groups; it was highly ranked by the poor. The poor also value highly *a comfortable life.* Other values more characteristic of the poor were *salvation, true friendship, being cheerful, helpful, obedient,* and *polite.* The affluent valued more highly a *sense of accomplishment, family security, inner harmony, mature love, wisdom, capable, imaginative, intellectual,* and *logical.*

Although there are many parallels between our findings and those of Rokeach, our data suggest that when studying family values the issue of family competence must be considered as well as socioeconomic status and ethnicity. The high correlation between the rankings for terminal values for the most competent black working-class families and the previously studied competent, affluent white families can be interpreted in many ways. One interpretation involves the adoption of middle-class values by successful working-class families as part of their assimilation into the mainstream of society. However, since the values underlying the continuance of family competence (i.e., autonomy, stability, etc.) can be seen as part of that mainstream, the interrelationship between values, family processes, and culturally defined success is difficult to untangle. Longitudinal family studies would help to clarify these complex relationships.

CHILDREARING PRACTICES

We were interested in finding previously published reports about childrearing practices and the processes of socialization and the establishment of a sense of autonomous self in children in families similar to those we studied. Goodman and Berman[65] provide a vividly descriptive account of children of the struggling poor in their paper "Tract Town Children." They note that in this very poor neighborhood child play is commonly characterized by fighting, and discipline by frequent "whippings." Mothers are authoritarian in their approach to their children, pushing them toward early autonomy, but then punishing them corporally for transgressions. The children express strong loyalty and affection for their mothers, suggesting that she is the center of the family. "She assigns chores, sees homework, metes out punishment, and warns against hazards" (p. 205). Many of the homes in this neighborhood do not have a father in them, but even in those homes with both parents father is much less important to these children. The children's aspirations for themselves tend to be high, but unrealistic. It is difficult to determine what the parents' aspirations are for their children. Children's fanciful wishes are either for material things or extravagant self-gratifications such as "I want to be a king" (p. 212).

Some of the most competent families in our sample came from neighborhoods as poor, hectic, and chaotic as Tract Town; yet these families and their children do not resemble those described by Goodman and Berman. For example, their aspirations seemed realistic and attainable. Their parents' aspirations for them were clearly defined and concordant with the children's aspirations. Children's wishes were related to the good of the family. Whereas children most commonly identified their mothers as the parent with whom they were closest, they also felt their fathers were an important influence in their lives. There was expressed affection, and good behavior was achieved through discussion, guidance, or punishment. Movement of children toward autonomy seemed guided and graduated. However, there are important similarities between the Tract Town families' childrearing behavior and those of the least competent and more impoverished families in our sample.

McGoldrick defines a number of issues in black families.[66] She addresses the high value placed on children by most black parents, and reviews an earlier work (Davis and Havighurst[67]) which suggests that black parents are lenient regarding weaning and feeding, but demanding regarding toilet training. However, she notes more recent studies (Allen,[22,68] Radin and Kamii,[69] Scanzoni[39]) that suggest that black/white childrearing practices are becoming similar. Black families tend to treat boys and girls much alike throughout childhood. McGoldrick makes the interesting point that disciplining of children is often strict and direct, but with good reasons. It is harder for black parents to protect their children or adolescents from severe consequences imposed by society when they act out. In this sense they are disciplined for their own protection. The most competent adolescents in our sample saw the fact that their parents were strict as a source of family strength.

Kamii and Radin[70] compared the socialization practices of middle- and lower-class Negro mothers. They found that, although childrearing goals do not differ, the processes do. Lower-class mothers are less responsive to the socioemotional needs of their children. They also spontaneously initiate fewer interactions with children than do middle-class black mothers. Lower-class mothers have a much less sophisticated repertoire of techniques for shaping or enforcing behavior, but still use positive reinforcement of good behavior as middle-class mothers do.

Bartz and Levine[71] compared and contrasted practices in a large number of black, white, and Mexican-American families living in a lower working-class neighborhood. In addition to the advantage of having a large sample, the authors use a rigorous methodology to assess seven qualities: control, support, permissiveness, strictness, egalitarianism, accelerated development, and "time press." Black parents are more controlling of their children, particularly sons, suggesting that boys need control and guidance to achieve high parental expectations. Black parents demonstrate the highest levels of support for their children. They are not significantly different from the other two groups with regard to permissiveness or strictness, but they demonstrated (as do Anglo parents) high degrees of support for egalitarian parent/child decision-making. Black parents press harder for accelerated development and are the most concerned about a child's wasting time.

There was not specific focus in our study on childrearing practices, and sophisticated assessment of these issues was beyond the scope of the project. However, we were impressed with the firm but supportive and understanding push of children toward responsible autonomy. The concern about keeping children busy in meaningful activities was particularly apparent in the most competent families.

BLACK ADOLESCENTS

Nolle[72] followed 278 Southern black adolescents over a three-year period to note any changes in perceived orientation toward parents and closeness, openness, respect, and susceptibility to moral influence. Two basic findings emerged: 1) Black sons and daughters showed little change on most dimensions over the time period, and 2) they did, however, feel less close to their fathers over time. The author interprets this finding as follows: "Since fathers play primarily instrumental roles within the family while mothers play primarily socioemotional ones, these changes possibly reflected the sloughing of a low priority role by the father in anticipation of the adolescent's disengagement from the family through his high school graduation" (p. 445). We did not gather data to document or refute this idea in our own sample.

The survey of black adolescents in a Southern metropolis by Coyners, Farmer, and Levin[62] reviews social and demographic characteristics and adds to our knowledge about self-image. These adolescents seem content, and 74% would make few or no changes in themselves. They have high levels of personal aspirations; 96% plan to stay in high school until graduation. Nearly half plan to go to college. When they need advice they most commonly turn to mother (57% ranked her first, 53% of males and 60% of females). The confidant preferred next is a personal friend of the same age. Only 12% seek advice from father. These adolescents advocate full integration and equality with whites. They are fairly religious, but do not seek advice commonly from a pastor, and few are "engulfed" by religion. The similarities of attitudes and orientations of the teenagers surveyed in this sample with those interviewed individually in our sample are clear.

One difference between the adolescents in this sample and the previously studied affluent white adolescents is the emergence of active heterosexual activity at younger ages in the black youths. Does the literature also reflect this finding? Do nonproblem black adolescents show early interest in and involvement in sexual behavior? Staples and

Mirande[1] call for the development of a systematic approach to black dating and sexual codes. Bell[73] states the black male "tends to learn about coitus at an earlier age than the white male" (p. 79), although Bell does not believe that there are any remarkable black/white differences with regard to sexual practices. He also calls for further study of this subject and says, "Finally, I suppose that I am more impressed by our ignorance . . . than by the capsule of knowledge which we possess" (p. 80). Broderick[74] surveyed 1,262 fifth through 12th grade adolescents and found that early in adolescence Negro boys are significantly more heterosexually oriented than white boys; the difference continues until ages 14–15 when the white youth catches up with his black counterpart. White girls were more heterosexually oriented than black girls across the teenage years except for ages 10–11, perhaps reflecting earlier pubescence in black girls. It should be noted that Broderick is describing heterosexual orientation (boyfriend/girlfriend relationships), not engagement in sexual intercourse.

ASPIRATIONS

The individuals in our study spoke often about aspirations for achievement and improvement of status in life, most often through education. These statements were common in the most competent families. Scanzoni[39] notes the expectation that children can achieve higher status. Hill[19] writes that high achievement orientation is one of the unheralded strengths of lower-income black families, and that methodological weaknesses of many studies of these families have caused researchers to overlook this fact. Rokeach's[64] assessment of values demonstrates that black people rank the value *ambition* highly. Coyners and coworkers[62] report high levels of educational aspirations in a large sample of urban adolescents. Bell[73] compares aspirations for their children by low and high social status black mothers. The high status mothers had occupational aspirations which were higher than those of the low status mothers, but even the low status mothers expected their children to advance. Parker and Kleiner[59] also show correlation between expectations for educational achievement and higher socioeconomic status, but they also report robust expectations in lower socioeconomic groups.

TIME ORIENTATION

We were interested in whether there might be a different orientation toward time and its usage in our group of research families. Lager[75] worked clinically with low-income, black, ghetto residents who were of lower income than our sample. He found more concern with time in its present perspective, with concerns about immediate survival, physical and psychological, than he did with time in its future perspective. There was little concern for the future or preparation for it. The study of Bartz and Levine[71] mentioned above demonstrated that black, lower-class mothers were more concerned than their white or Mexican-American counterparts that their children not waste time. In our sample of families there was both a concern for the effective use of time and planning for the future. The recognition of present and future time as valuable assets seems to be more acute in the more competent families.

KINSHIP BONDS

Hill[19] notes that strong kinship bonds are a strength that black families have evolved through the course of turbulent history. McAdoo[76] studied a group of middle-income black families and supports a hypothesis that "high levels of interaction would be found in all families in which family members are within visiting distance . . . " (p. 775). She also supports a hypothesis that "families who were born working-class would have higher reciprocal obligation expectations than families who were born middle-class . . . " (p. 774). Yost[63] compared middle- and lower-class black families and found that those with lower income place higher importance on kin relationships and those with higher income place higher importance on friend relationships. Bagarozzi,[25] whose concern is the best approach to therapy with black families, emphasizes the importance of the extended family and includes them in therapy sessions when indicated.

We made no attempt to quantify rigorously kin interactions or reciprocal obligations for the families in our sample. We were not impressed, however, with any kin interactions which would be unusual in families of other ethnic or socioeconomic groups. One trend, however, was an attitude of independence and self-sufficiency in the families in our sample rated as most competent. This finding is comparable to that of McQueen's[33] study demonstrating that one difference between impoverished black families' effective and noneffective coping was strong self-reliance during times of severe economic deprivation rather than borrowing from friends or relatives.

RELIGION

The church is the most commonly referenced support system in the literature on black families. Hill[19] believes that church affiliation is one of the paramount strengths of black families and that such has been true since slavery days. The church was a major source of power for civil rights advocacy several decades ago. Comstock and Partridge,[77] who gathered data from individuals of different ethnic and socioeconomic levels, suggest that frequent church attenders have better physical health. Their study does not, however, attend to the issue of what a central influence the church can be in the lives of black people. The church is a primary support of black society. Hill[19] quotes an advocate of the black church, "Whatever you want to do in the Negro community, whether it's selling Easter Seals or organizing a nonviolent campaign, you've got to do it through the Negro church or it doesn't get done" (p. 35). Edwards[78] suggests that affiliation with the church as a guiding political as well as moral power is strong, even for those embracing nontraditional sects. McGoldrick,[66] in a recent work on normal family processes, suggests that most blacks turn to religion as a solution to their problems before they think of psychotherapy. Griffith and colleagues[79,80] present moving descriptive accounts of the power of a religious service in a black church to heal and guide.

One important question is whether religion is used differentially by black families depending on their socioeconomic status or degree of competence. Willie,[34] in his comparison of families in three groups (middle-class, working-class, and lower-class), found differences. He found religion likely to be important to all, but his middle- and working-class families, while attending church with a frequency ranging from occasionally to regularly, did not show the extreme responses of either avoidance or religious "engulfment" seen in the lower-class

families. In their contrast of "problem" and "stable" families in the
low-income housing project, Willie and Weinandy[32] do not comment
on a different use of religion between the two groups. However,
McQueen,[33] in his comparison of coping and noncoping poor, black
families, found the former group characterized by a "quest for respectability" which was most commonly achieved through active church
participation.

Our data suggest the need to consider both socioeconomic status and
family competence in studying the role of religion in black family life.
For the more competent families, religion was a central aspect of family
life, whereas such was not so for the least competent families. However,
the differences in family income between the two groups makes interpretation difficult. Longitudinal studies with larger samples will help
to sort out the relationships between family competence, religion, and
socioeconomic status.

MARITAL RELATIONSHIPS

With regard to power distribution between parents, a focus shared
by family systems theoreticians and students of the black family has
developed. Family systems researchers focus on power as one of the
key variables in assessing families. Investigators of black family life
also commented repeatedly about distribution of power, but perhaps
for a different reason. It will be remembered that the Moynihan report
stimulated researchers to gather data to refute Moynihan's primary as-
sertions that the black family is matriarchal in nature. Hill points out
that Moynihan based this assertion on the findings of one study (Blood
and Wolfe[44]), but misinterpreted their data. Although black partners
show a slight skew toward dominance of the wife on a "power" scale
as compared to white couples, the average scores for both were egalitarian. In any case, those who study and comment on black families
have paid particular attention to the issue of conjugal power. Hyman
and Reed,[81] Middleton and Putney,[82] Aldous,[83] Allen,[68] Jackson,[84] Billingsley,[16] Deitrick,[85] Scanzoni,[39] Heiss,[31] and Willie and Greenblat[36]
emphasize the role of egalitarian marital patterns in black families.
King[86] approaches the question by gathering the perception of parents'
power by ninth grade teenagers: Boys tend to see father as more power-

ful, girls see mother more so, but both perceive a basically egalitarian distribution. These studies, underscoring shared parental power, rely either on interviews or a pencil-and-paper format. Mack[87] used these techniques, but added a bargaining task in order to assess who held power directly. She compared black and white couples of both middle- and working-classes. From the questionnaire, working-class husbands were relatively more powerful, but there were no significant differences when the partners were assessed by the other two methods. Our judgments about the distribution of marital power were made on the basis of our ratings from the direct observation of marital and family interactions. They rely less on what the participants say about the distribution of power than on how the participants interact with each other. Who decides who is to speak, who interrupts whom, and who can change the subject are some of the criteria upon which our ratings of power distribution are made.

Our findings emphasize the equal power of the marital relationships in the most competent black families. Strongly skewed or conflicted marital relationships are characteristic of the least competent families, but not of the sample as a whole.

A major difference between the most competent working-class black families and the previously studied more affluent white families is the failure of the parents in the former group to demonstrate the level of intimate communication found in the parents in the earlier sample. Although there are confirming studies in the literature, the issue is complicated by the use of different definitions of marital intimacy. The most commonly used concepts are those of marital expressiveness and marital satisfaction. These appear to be broader concepts than our use of the concept of intimate communication.

Expressiveness, as it applies to the whole family, was not significantly different in the working- and middle-class samples. Both the most competent working-class and most competent middle-class families expressed a wide range of feelings, were clear in communicating, and demonstrated moderately high levels of empathy. The difference between the two groups occurs only in the parental relationship and is specifically concerned with a deeper and more vulnerable level of communication.

Renne, for example, finds that black spouses report lower levels of marital satisfaction than do whites.[41] The diminished levels of marital satisfaction are related to lower family income and larger family size. Willie[88] summarizes his studies by suggesting that the cohesion of the black working-class family is more the result of the parents' heroic joint effort to stave off adversity than of their shared understanding and tenderness. In a well-controlled study, Henggeler and Tavormina[89] found that the diminished warmth and affection in both lower-class black and white families may be a direct reflection of differences in verbal IQs and family size.

Scanzoni[39] states that the evidence linking the occupational status, education, and income of the husband to the spouses' evaluations of expressive aspects of their marriages is very strong. He suggests that a social exchange perspective is useful in understanding linkages. In this view, the husband's provision of adequate entry into the economic-opportunity structure directly influences the wife's provision of empathy and other expressive satisfactions. To the extent that the wife feels alienated from the economic-opportunity structure, the less empathic she will be and the greater the likelihood that both spouses will report diminished expressive satisfaction. Scanzoni's work documents the crucial role that socioeconomic deprivation plays in altering the structure and function of the family.

In summary, there is much support in the literature for the major findings of this study, but the issue of differing levels of family competence within any ethnic or socioeconomic group has not been sufficiently attended. We believe that doing so clarifies some of the contradictions in the black family literature and leads to a series of further hypotheses that will shed light on important dimensions of family life in general.

REFERENCES

1. Staples, R., & Mirande, A. Racial and cultural variations among American families: A decennial review of the literature on minority families. *Journal of Marriage and the Family,* November, 1980, 887–903.
2. Moynihan, D. P. *The Negro family: The case for national action.* Office of Policy Planning and Research, U.S. Department of Labor, 1965.
3. X, Cedrik (Clark). The role of the white researcher in black society: A futuristic look. *Journal of Social Issues,* 1973, *29*(1), 109–118.

4. Nobles, W. W. Toward an empirical and theoretical framework for defining black families. *Journal of Marriage and the Family,* November, 1978, 679–688.

5. Merton, R. K. Insiders and outsiders: A chapter in the sociology of knowledge. *American Journal of Sociology,* July, 1972, *78,* 9–48.

6. Sawyer, E. Methodological problems in studying so-called "deviant" communities. In J. A. Ladner, *Death of white sociology.* Westminister, Maryland: Random House, 1973.

7. Mathis, A. Contrasting approaches to the study of black families. *Journal of Marriage and the Family,* November, 1978, 667–676.

8. Frazier, E. F. *The Negro family in the United States.* Chicago: University of Chicago Press, 1939.

9. Rainwater, L. *Family design.* Chicago: Aldine, 1965.

10. Rainwater, L. Crucible of identity: The Negro lower-class family. In T. Parsons & K. B. Clark (Eds.), *The Negro American.* Boston: Beacon Press, 1965, 160–204.

11. Bernard, J. *Marriage and family among Negros.* Englewood Cliffs, N.J.: Prentice Hall, 1966.

12. Parker, S., & Kleiner, R. Characteristics of Negro mothers and single-headed households. *Journal of Marriage and the Family,* November, 1966, *28,* 507–513.

13. Blood, R., & Wolfe, D. Negro-white differences in blue collar marriages in a Northern metropolis. *Social Forces,* September, 1969, *48,* 59–64.

14. Herskovits, M. J. *The myth of the Negro past.* Boston: Beacon Press, 1958.

15. Blassingame, J. W. *The slave community: Plantation life in Annie Bellam's South.* New York: Oxford Press, 1972.

16. Billingsley, A. *Black families in white America.* Englewood Cliffs, N.J.: Prentice Hall, 1968.

17. Young, V. H. Family and childhood in a Southern Negro community. *American Anthropologist,* September, 1970, *72,* 269–288.

18. Young, V. H. A black American socialization pattern. *American Ethnologist,* May, 1974, *1,* 405–413.

19. Hill, R. *The strengths of black families.* New York: Emerson-Hall, 1972.

20. Nobles, W. W. Africanity: Its role in black families. *The Black Scholar,* June, 1974, *5,* 10–17.

21. Turnbull, C. M. *Man in Africa.* Garden City, New York: Anchor Press/Doubleday, 1976.

22. Allen, W. R. The search for applicable theories of black family life. *Journal of Marriage and the Family,* February, 1978, 117–129.

23. Staples, R. Toward a sociology of the black family: A theoretical and methodological assessment. *Journal of Marriage and the Family,* February, 1971, 119–138.

24. Rainwater, L. Crucible of identity: The lower class Negro family. *Daedalus,* Winter, 1966, *95,* 172–216.

25. Bagarozzi, D. A. Family therapy and the black middle-class: A neglected area of study. *Journal of Marital and Family Therapy,* April, 1980, 159–166.

26. Haley, J. Problem solving therapy. San Francisco: Jossey-Bass, 1976.

27. Haley, J. The family of the schizophrenic: A model system. *American Journal of Nervous and Mental Disorders,* 1959, *129,* 357–374.

28. Jackson, J. J. Family organization and ideology. In K. S. Miller & R. M. Dreger

(Eds.), *Comparative studies of blacks and whites in the United States*. New York: Seminar Press, 1973.

29. Lewis, J. M., Beavers, W. R., Gossett, J. T., & Phillips, V. A. *No single thread: Psychological health in family systems*. New York: Brunner/Mazel, 1977.
30. Willie, C. V. *Family life of black people*. Columbus, Ohio: Charles V. Merrill, 1970.
31. Heiss, J. *The case of the black family: A sociological inquiry*. New York: Columbia University Press, 1975.
32. Willie, C. V., & Weinandy, J. The structure and compostion of "problem" and "stable" families in a low-income population. In C. V. Willie (Ed.), *The family life of black people*. Columbus, Ohio: Charles E. Merrill, 1970.
33. McQueen, A. J. *The adaptations of urban black families: Trends, problems, and issues*. Presented at the Conference on Families in Contemporary America: Varieties of Form, Function, and Experience. Sponsored by the Department of Psychiatry and Behavioral Sciences, George Washington University School of Medicine and the Center for Continuing Education in Mental Health, Psychiatric Institute Foundation, June, 10, 11, 1977, Washington, D.C.
34. Willie, C. V. The black family and social class. *American Journal of Orthopsychiatry*, January, 1974, *44*, 50–60.
35. Willie, C. V. Family life among the poor in the Cardozo area of Washington, D.C. In C. V. Willie (Ed.), *Family life of black people*. Columbus, Ohio: Charles E. Merrill, 1970, 197–202.
36. Willie, C. V., & Greenblatt, S. L. Four "classic" studies of power relationships in black families: A review and look to the future. *Journal of Marriage and the Family*, November, 1978, 691–694.
37. Willie, C. V. *A new look at black families*. Bayside, New York: General Hall, 1976.
38. Willie, C. V. Intergenerational poverty. In C. V. Willie (Ed.), *The family life of black people*. Columbus, Ohio: Charles E. Merrill, 1970, 316–330.
39. Scanzoni, J. H. *The black family in modern society: Patterns of stability and security*. Chicago: The University of Chicago Press, 1977.
40. Scanzoni, J. H. Sex roles, economic factors, and marital solidarity in black and white marriages. *Journal of Marriage and the Family*, February, 1975, 130–144.
41. Renne, K. S. Correlates of dissatisfaction in marriage. *Journal of Marriage and the Family*, February, 1970, 54–67.
42. Bell, R. R. The related importance of mother and wife roles among black lower-class women. In R. Staples (Ed.), *The black family: Essays and studies*. Belmont, California: Wadsworth Publishing Co., Inc. 1978, 248–255.
43. Galligan, R. J., & Bahr, S. J. Economic well-being and marital stability: Implications for income maintenance programs. *Journal of Marriage and the Family*, May, 1978, *40*, 283–290.
44. Blood, R. O., Jr., & Wolfe, D. M. Negro-white differences in blue-collar marriages in a Northern metropolis. In R. Staples (Ed.), *The black family: Essays and studies*. Belmont, California: Wadsworth Publishing Co., Inc., 1978, 171–178.
45. McGee, D. P. White conditioning of black dependency. *Journal of Social Issues*, 1973, *29*(1), 53–56.

46. Nobles, W. W. Psychological research and the black self-concept: A critical review. *Journal of Social Issues,* 1973, *29*(1), 11–31.
47. Adelson, J. A. A study of minority group authoritarianism. *Journal of Abnormal and Social Psychology,* 1953, *48,* 477–485.
48. Radke-Yarrow, M., & Lande, B. Personality correlates of minority group belonging. *Journal of Social Psychology,* 1953, *38,* 253–272.
49. Sarnoff, I. Identification with the aggressor: Some personality correlates of anti-semitism among Jews. *Journal of Personality,* 1951, *20,* 199–218.
50. Clark, K. B., & Clark, M. P. Racial identification and preference in Negro Children. In T. M. Newcomb & E. L. Hartley (Eds.), *Readings in social psychology.* New York: Holt, Rinehart, & Winston, 1947.
51. Stevenson, H. W. & Stewart, E. C. A developmental study of racial awareness in young children. *Child Development,* 1958, *29,* 399–410.
52. Radke, M., & Trager, H. E. Children's perceptions of the social roles of Negros and whites. *Journal of Psychology,* 1950, *29,* 3–33.
53. Goodman, M. E. *Race awareness in young children.* Reading, MA.: Addison-Wesley, 1952.
54. Moreland, J. K. Racial recognition by nursery school children in Lynchburg, Virginia. *Social Forces,* 1958, *37,* 132–137.
55. Landreth, C., & Johnson, B. C. Young children's responses to picture and inset test design to reveal reactions to persons of different skin color. *Child Development,* 1953, *24,* 63–79.
56. Grossack, M. Group belongingness among Negros. *Journal of Social Psychology,* 1956, *43,* 167–180.
57. Noel, D. L. Group identification among Negros: An empirical analysis. *Journal of Social Issues,* 1964, *20*(2), 71–84.
58. Sewad, G. *Psychotherapy and culture conflict.* New York: Ronald Press, 1956.
59. Parker, S., & Kleiner, R. J. *Mental illness in the urban Negro community.* New York: Free Press, 1965.
60. Proshansky, H., & Newton, P. The nature and meaning of Negro self-identity. In M. Deutsch, I. Katz, & A. R. Jensen (Eds.), *Social class, race, and psychological development.* New York: Holt, Rinehart, & Winston, 1968.
61. Rodman, H. The lower-class value stretch. *Social Forces,* 1963, *42,* 205–215.
62. Coyners, J. E., Farmer, W. F., & Levin, M. L. Black youth in a Southern metropolis. In C. Willie, *The family life of black people.* Columbus, Ohio: Charles E. Merrill, 1970.
63. Yost, J. A. *The relative function of kin: A comparative study of middle and lower-class black families.* University of Colorado, Ph.D. Dissertation, 1973. University Microfilms International, Ann Arbor, Michigan. L–275492–88.
64. Rokeach, M. *The nature of human values.* New York: The Free Press, 1973.
65. Goodman, M. E., & Berman, A. Tract Town Children. In C. Willie (Ed.), *The family life of black people.* Columbus, Ohio: Merrill Publishing Company, 1970, 203–215.
66. McGoldrick, M. Normal families: An ethnic perspective. In F. Walsh (Ed.), *Normal family processes.* New York: The Guilford Press, 1982, 399–424.
67. Davis, A., & Havighurst, R. Social class and color differences in child rearing. *American Sociological Review,* 1946, *11,*698–710.

68. Allen, W. R. Black family research in the United States: A review, assessment, and extension. *Journal of Comparative Family Studies,* 1978, *9,* 166–188.
69. Radin, N., & Kamii, C. The child rearing attitudes of disadvantaged Negro mothers and some educational implications. *Journal of Negro Education,* 1965, *34,* 138–146.
70. Kamii, C., & Radin, N. Class differences in the socialization practices of Negro mothers. *Journal of Marriage and the Family,* 1967, *29,* 302–312.
71. Bartz, K. W., & Levine, E. S. Child rearing by black parents: A description and comparison to Anglo and Chicago parents. *Journal of Marriage and the Family,* 1978, 709–719.
72. Nolle, D. B. Changes in black sons and daughters: A panel analysis of black adolescents' orientations towards their parents. *Journal of Marriage and the Family,* August, 1972, 443–447.
73. Bell, R. B. Lower-class Negro mothers' aspirations for their children. *Social Forces,* 1965, *43,* 493–500.
74. Broderick, C. B. Social and heterosexual development among urban Negros and whites. *Journal of Marriage and the Family,* 1965, *27,* 200–203.
75. Lager, E. *Time orientation and psychotherapy in the ghetto.* Presented at the 132nd Annual Meeting of the American Psychiatric Association, Chicago, May, 1979.
76. McAdoo, H. P. Factors related to stability in upwardly mobile black families. *Journal of Marriage and the Family,* November, 1978, 761–776.
77. Comstock, G. W., & Partridge, K. B. Church attendance and health. *Journal of Chronic Disease,* 1972, *25,* 665–672.
78. Edwards, H. Black Muslim and Negro Christian family relationship. *Journal of Marriage and the Family,* 1968, *30,* 604–611.
79. Griffith, E. H., & Mathewson, M. E. *Communitas and charisma in a black church service.* Presented at the 133rd Annual Meeting of the American Psychiatric Association. San Francisco, May, 1980.
80. Griffith, E. H., English, T., & Mayfield, V. Possession, prayer, and testimony: Therapeutic aspects of the Wednesday night meeting in a black church. *Psychiatry,* 1980, *43,* 120–128.
81. Hyman, H. H., & Reed, J. S. Black matriarchy reconsidered: Evidence from secondary analysis of sample surveys. *Public Opinion Quarterly,* 1969, *33,* 346–354.
82. Middleton, R., & Putney, S. Dominance in decisions in the family: Race and class differences. In C. V. Willie (Ed.), *The family life of black people.* Columbus, Ohio: Charles E. Merrill Publishing Company, 1970, 16–22.
83. Aldous, J. Wives' employment status and lower-class men as husband-fathers: Support for the Moynihan thesis. *Journal of Marriage and the Family,* August, 1969, 469–476.
84. Jackson, L. B. The attitudes of black females towards upper- and lower-class black males. *Journal of Black Psychology,* 1975, *1,* 53–64.
85. Deitrick, T. A re-examination of the myth of black matriarchy. *Journal of Marriage and the Family,* May, 1975, 367–374.
86. King, A. Adolescent perception of power structure in the Negro family. *Journal of Marriage and the Family,* November, 1969, 751–756.

146   The Long Struggle

87. Mack, D. The power relationship in black families and white families. *Journal of Personality and Social Psychology*, 1974, *39*(3), 409–413.
88. Willie, C. V. The black family and social class. *American Journal of Orthopsychiatry,* January, 1974, *44*, 50–60.
89. Henggeler, S. W., & Tavormina, J. B. Social class and race differences in family interaction: Pathological, normative, or confounding methodological factors? *Journal of Genetic Psychology*, 1980, *137*, 211–222.

CHAPTER 9

Implications for Research and Clinical Practice

The findings of this study have implications for both research and clinical practice, although the small size of the sample restricts the breadth of generalizations that can be made. We wish to emphasize that the 18 families were studied intensively with a variety of both family and individual measures, resulting in a picture of each family which is rich and "deep." Although we strive for a balance of the more structured techniques with those that explore pertinent leads without the imposition of a fixed structure, we have been impressed, as in our previous work, with the capacity of techniques designed to measure interactions among family members to go beyond what family members are able or willing to tell us about their families.

The research process — from conceptualizing to data analysis — does not appear to have been influenced by the ethnicity of the researchers. Whether it involved scoring family interactional tapes, rating individual interview transcripts, or conducting interviews in the field, there was statistically significant agreement between black and white members of the research team. With the exception, however, of one black professional who grew up poor, all members of the research team had middle-class backgrounds. If the process of our research has a consistent bias, it is more likely that it is a social class perspective rather than one that follows ethnic lines.

Another issue involves the focus on intact families. The need for this criterion was based on the nature of the major research hypothesis. Selecting single-parent families, however responsive to social circumstances, would have obscured adequate comparison of this sample of families with their more affluent counterparts. The study of single-parent families, we believe, requires different perspectives and procedures. Competence in such families may require very different combinations of variables than does competence in two-parent families.

THE CONTINUUM OF FAMILY COMPETENCE

Before proceeding to discuss the implications of our findings for research and clinical activities, it seems appropriate to emphasize again the utility of the Continuum of Family Competence as a way of ordering a wide variety of families along dimensions that have implications for both research and clinical endeavors. Although many family clinicians and researchers utilize the same variables in their work with families, there is little evidence of movement toward a shared nosology. Rather, those colleagues who believe that attempts at systematic classification (however constantly in revision) move the field in a preferred and useful direction tend to use either their own system or that learned from an influential teacher. Those colleagues who eschew any efforts at classification are, in our experience, more apt to see each family as unique and each treatment effort as an uncharted adventure. We believe the evolution of a broadly accepted family nosology is basic to the careful assessment of family strengths and problems which, in turn, can lead to the application of specific clinical techniques to particular family problems.

It is also necessary to emphasize that we consider the Continuum of Family Competence an evolving nosology, of which only the skeletal structure is currently in place. As experience expands, distinctions between subgroups of families will be clarified at each basic point on the continuum. Clinically, for example, there is evidence that in dominant-submissive dysfunctional families the degree to which the skewed parental power distribution is complementary may offer an important distinction between two subgroups of this type of family. Beavers, so much a part of the research team during our early studies, presents data suggesting that the distinction between centrifugal and centripetal dimensions of family systems may offer another refinement of the Continuum of Family Competence.[1] Other improvements are anticipated and should add to the utility of the continuum.

We use the Continuum of Family Competence in clinical endeavors as an initial, orienting conceptualization of a family. Although it provides certain basic guidelines for the type of intervention procedures most likely to be helpful, it is not a complete assessment of the family. After a family's location on the continuum is defined, the clinician moves to a more microscopic focus and searches for family characteristics that distinguish the family from other families at a similar level of competence. In this regard, use of the continuum is comparable to the use of DSM-III with individual patients. Establishing a DSM-III diagnosis of a borderline personality disorder, for example, is but the initial step in the search for understanding. More data are needed in order to ascertain what type or level of borderline disturbance the patient is experiencing.

One of the strengths of the Continuum of Family Competence as a beginning nosological system is its base in systematically collected research data with established reliability of raters' judgments.

The current project extends the generalizability of the continuum beyond middle- and upper-middle-class families. The demonstration that the continuum distinguishes accurately families of different levels of competence in a lower-income working-class sample is an important step. It is equally important to determine its applicability in other groups of families as, for example, those who live with even greater economic deprivation.

IMPLICATIONS FOR RESEARCH

In addition to the ways in which the Continuum of Family Competence lends itself to a variety of research hypotheses, there are a number of both general and specific issues that need emphasis and clarification. At the most general level, the study underscores the urgent need for further family systems research. One of the several general areas to which we would assign high priority is the need for systematic longitudinal research using interactional measurement techniques. The use of the Continuum of Family Competence, for example, evaluates the level of competence of a family at the time of observation. It does not, however, explain *how* a family reached a particular level of competence. Studying families over time would provide a developmental perspective. Whether well-functioning families at different stages of family development demonstrate similar system characteristics is a question to be answered empirically. Current family theory predicts that system characteristics will change in response to the developmental challenges of different periods of family life. This important concept needs the test of predictive studies. In a similar manner, current family theory predicts that the successful management of family developmental challenges of a particular period is dependent on the successful accomplishment of the tasks associated with earlier developmental periods, the concept of epigenesis. To our knowledge, there are no empirical data with which to confirm this intriguing concept.

At a different level, we do not know whether family development is similar for different socioeconomic and ethnic groups. The data from this project suggest that earlier periods in the lives of this sample of families may have required far more struggle, particularly in the development of instrumental or management skills, and that this struggle may have delayed or interfered with the development of marital intimacy. This interpretation, however, is made from individual retrospective accounts of earlier days rather than direct measurement of marital or family system characteristics. It may, therefore, reflect retrospective distortion. Longitudinal family studies would help to clarify such an important issue.

A second important need is for what might be called "cross-domain" family studies. For example, few family studies include measurement of biological variables. Reiss emphasizes the need for such research designs in the study of schizophrenia.[2] Our experience suggests that the choice of which biological variables to measure is difficult, but collaboration with biologically oriented colleagues can be helpful. Recent work on the apparent interaction of a family system characteristic, Expressed Emotion, and a family member's response to psychotropic agents suggests the importance of cross-domain studies.[3,4,5]

Another crucial area for family research is the relationship of family system characteristics to the development of major psychiatric syn-

dromes in family members. Whether family variables play predisposing, precipitating, or sustaining roles (or all three) in any, some, or
all major psychiatric syndromes can be clarified by longitudinal, cross-
domain family studies.

An area of general concern emphasized in our earlier work involves
the hazards to research efforts in considering control groups as homo-
geneous.[6] Both the current study and the earlier report regarding
middle- and upper-middle-class white families demonstrate that intact
families of similar demographic characteristics in which no family
member has a clearly diagnosable psychiatric syndrome vary tremendously in levels of family competence. To assume that such families are
alike or "normal" invites erroneous interpretations. If, for example,
one contrasts families of clinical interest with a control group of families selected, as not uncommonly, on the basis of the absence of a major
psychiatric syndrome in a family member, one does not know the level
of competence of the control families; if the control group is skewed
with dysfunctional families, for example, the differences between the
control group and the target group may be minimized.

In addition to these general areas, the findings from this study suggest the need for further research in a number of more specific areas.
Perhaps more than any other issue, this study points out the need to
explore further the heterogeneity of families at a particular socioeconomic level. This study demonstrates that the concept of working-class,
two-parent black families is such a broad description that it tells us
very little. At this particular socioeconomic level there are very different groups of families. One group, the most competent, is more like
a comparable group of middle- and upper-middle-class white families
than like their less competent neighbors of similar socioeconomic
status. Studies clarifying the heterogeneity of other types of families
are obviously needed.

Another specific area involves the impact of socioeconomic and ethnic factors on the development of marital intimacy. If intimacy is defined as a level of communication involving the reciprocal sharing of
thoughts, feelings, hopes, fears, and fantasies concerning which the
individual feels some sense of vulnerability, the working-class black
parents in this sample of families did not reveal that level of communication. This is a sharp contrast to the more affluent white parents

in our earlier sample, for whom this level of trusting openness was a central feature of the marital relationship. This difference between the two samples merits further exploration. The major clue available is present primarily in the retrospective accounts of the wives. In recalling the early days of their marriages, they describe a period of turmoil and confusion as neither spouse had the skills necessary to manage their marginal economic circumstances. Their mutual struggle and ultimate success in surviving, establishing an economic foothold, starting a family, purchasing a modest home, and generating an income to assure the survival of the family were the elements of their relationship which they reported with greatest pride. The suggestion that such struggles may preclude or delay the development of marital intimacy is strengthened by the fact that the affluent white parents did not describe an early period characterized by the painful search for the necessary management skills. Their middle-class backgrounds and college educations appear to have provided them with the requisite management skills to deal with a much more favorable economic context, and it seems reasonable to hypothesize that the presence of such favorable circumstances provided them with the freedom to experiment with and develop patterns of intimate marital communication.

A second factor described by a number of the wives (and some of the husbands) was the husband's "wildness" during the initial years of the marriage. The use of this term by a number of the subjects involved a common pattern: the newly married male's continuing allegiance to his single male friends and his involvement with them in drinking and extramarital sexual exploits. "It took me several years to get him settled down" was stated by a number of the wives. Both the wives and husbands acknowledge that this settling into the marriage was frequently associated with a resurgence or development of religious activity on the part of the husband. Our more affluent sample of families did not describe such periods of "wildness," but rather a smooth transition into marital roles.

These findings also suggest that the development of marital intimacy may have been delayed or interfered with by these difficulties in the early years of the marriage. The hypothesis that working-class couples in general, or working-class black couples specifically, do not develop levels of marital intimacy because early in the relationship there are both insufficient shared management skills for their economically deprived situation and the husband's difficulty in settling into a conjugal role can be tested by appropriate longitudinal studies of young couples. Although anecdotal evidence suggests that marital intimacy may develop rapidly, slowly, or not at all, there remains the possibility that there are critical periods in the evolution of a marriage during which certain tasks must be accomplished or the probability of their later development is reduced. What role ethnic and socioeconomic variables play in such a developmental equation is not known, but our data suggest the role of intervening variables (management skills inadequate for a severely deprived context and the husband's "wildness") that may operate between socioeconomic or ethnic factors and marital intimacy. Scanzoni presents a related hypothesis in his exchange theory: The husband's provision of the necessary economic resources is responded to by the wife with high levels of affection (by inference, the context in which marital intimacy may develop).[7] Longitudinal family studies would help in clarifying whether such a paradigm operates in couples with marginal economic resources.

A third project involves exploring the complex relationship between family value orientations and family competence. A number of contemporary family theorists postulate that families derive their organizational structure from their need to elaborate and conserve a basic family value orientation. This process may have shared conscious components, but much of it is unspoken and presumably out of the consciousness of family members.

A second hypothesis suggests, rather, that the structural characteristics of a relationship are determined by factors other than value orientations, and that these relationship characteristics contribute to the evolution of a shared value orientation. Such either-or conceptualizations are simplifications of complex and reciprocal relationships in which, at the minimum, value orientations lead to relationship structure which, in turn, influences the continued evolution of value orientations.

A critical issue is the problem of determining family value orientations with methodological rigor and some promise of replicability. Spiegel[8] offers a conceptual format based on the work of Kluckhohn[9,10] that is helpful. It is based on the assumption that there are a limited number of universal problems for which all people must find some solutions: 1) time, the temporal focus of human life (past, present, or future); 2) activity, the preferred pattern of action in interpersonal relationships (doing, being, being-in-becoming); 3) relational orientation, the preferred way of relating in groups (individual, collateral, lineal); 4) man-nature orientation, the relationship to the natural or supernatural environment (harmony, mastery, subjugation); 5) and the basic nature of man, attitudes about the innate good or evil in men and women (neutral/mixed, good, evil).

Spiegel suggests that a society will contain all possible solutions but will be characterized by a dominant profile of first-order value choices along with second- and third-order substitutions. The current mainstream American middle-class dominant profile emphasizes the future, doing, the individual, mastery over nature, and a neutral orientation regarding the innate good or evil in men and women. This dominant, middle-class profile is understood to "exert the pull" toward which ethnic groups (and, we would add, lower socioeconomic groups) move.

It is clear from this format that our use of the concept of family competence is intimately involved with Spiegel's dominant profile of middle-class values. Families rated as most competent are those whose relationship processes can be inferred both to evolve from such a value orientation and to confirm its "correctness."

The relationship processes of the most competent working-class black families, so much like those of the previously studied more affluent white families, can be inferred to reflect the presence of Spiegel's dominant profile of middle-class value orientations. One problem, however, is the level of inference required in relating family processes to underlying value orientations. This is no more true, of course, for this sample of families than for any other sample. What are needed are independent assessments of family value orientations and of family relationship processes in order to reduce the degree of inference. Even this, however, will not necessarily clarify the ways in which family value orientations and family competence are related over time; longitudinal studies are required.

The use of the Rokeach Value Survey has many advantages, but it does not illuminate the type of value orientation that much family theory speaks to in terms of organizing paradigms. Rather, it deals with the issue of values at a more concrete level and provides not only comparisons between groups of families, but also data for building hypotheses. An example from this sample of families is the relationship between the religious value, *salvation,* and family competence. Whether this correlation reflects an underlying future orientation or other more complex relationships between religious beliefs and competent family functioning may be clarified by subsequent studies.

However, research projects aimed at clarifying the presumably complex relationships between family competence and family value orientation must take into consideration factors other than mainstream values that influence specific groups of families.

Pinderhughes,[11] for example, has suggested that the black ethnic identity is influenced by three cultural sources: residuals from Africa, identification with mainstream America, and adaptations and responses to the "victim" system that is a product of racism, poverty, and oppression. These three sources of black culture have very different values. Mainstream American values emphasize individualism, ownership of material goods, mastery, youth, and the future; African values stress collectivity, affiliation, sharing, obedience to authority, and spirituality; and the victim system values emphasize cooperation to combat powerlessness, strict obedience to an oppressive authority, strength, suppression of feelings into creative activities, spirituality, luck, and the present. Behavior based on victim-system values includes immediate gratification, manipulativeness, passive-aggressiveness, rebelliousness, and identification with the aggressor. These behaviors are seen as having adaptive value as responses to powerlessness, but are maladaptive for functioning in mainstream America.

Values from each of the three value systems are found in black families and may explain the wide diversity in family structure. Blacks experience strain in the attempt to cope with such conflicting values, and Pinderhughes stresses that they have not been presented with the opportunity of identifying exclusively with the mainstream culture. As a consequence, black individuals and families must live in several cultures simultaneously, often with considerable resulting stress. This stress is reinforced by the societal projection process[12] by which one group maintains its illusion of competence by ascribing to another group its own undesirable qualities. Under these combined stresses the black family may undergo significant structural change manifested, for example, by increasing rigidity, disorganization, or disintegration. In this regard Pinderhughes suggests the black family's response to the internal stresses of biculturality and the external stress of societal projection is in the same direction that we hypothesize to result from socioeconomic stress. Pinderhughes states, however, that some black families are able to become exceptionally clear about their identity and values and exhibit unusual strength. She suggests that middle-class black families have more resources with which to deal with the stress, but do not emerge unscathed. As is clear from Pinderhughes' insightful analysis, research aimed at clarifying the relationship between family competence and family value orientations must take into account the specific forces that influence the family value orientations of particular groups of families.

A final area for future research involves our major hypothesis regarding the impact of socioeconomic stress on family organization and function. To reiterate our major finding: Competent working-class black families demonstrated, with few exceptions, the same interactional patterns as more affluent and competent white counterparts. Within the sample, however, were families rated as clearly dysfunctional, with either a dominant-submissive or chronically conflicted family structure. These families had much lower family incomes than did the more competent black subjects. The data suggest a socioeconomic threshold below which the development of the characteristics associated with high levels of family competence may be improbable. A larger sample of families with incomes at or below the family size-adjusted poverty level is needed in order to test this hypothesis more rigorously. In our study the working-class black families with incomes $3,000 to $4,000 above the poverty level who achieve high levels of family competence are very similar to affluent and highly competent white families. It remains to be demonstrated, however, whether families living under harsher socioeconomic circumstances can achieve the type of family structure accomplished by their working-class neighbors.

This all presumes that the socioeconomic context has a decisive impact on what is possible in family life. To further untangle the reciprocal relationship between socioeconomic circumstances and family competence will require longitudinal family studies.

The research questions we have posed are but a few of the many that grow out of our work. Although certain types of questions can obviously be answered by cross-sectional designs, only longitudinal studies will clarify the ways in which complex variables interact over time and, in concert, produce families that either succeed or fail in the major tasks of family life.

IMPLICATIONS FOR CLINICAL ACTIVITIES

The usefulness of the Continuum of Family Competence as an initial, broad-brush approach to distinguishing families at different levels of competence has been articulated earlier. The data from this study of working-class black families extend that usefulness to another sample of families. Clinicians who choose to use this approach with families from either middle- and upper-middle-class white families or working-class black families have available a format that may assist in three related clinical endeavors: the recognition of the degree of family dysfunction, the establishment of treatment goals, and the applicability of specific techniques to families at different levels of competence.

Recognition of the degree of family dysfunction is an important orienting step for family clinicians. What needs emphasis, however, is that, after locating the zone on the continuum that describes a given family, the clinician then needs to consider whether a current stress has resulted in structural alterations within the family. This is regression under stress, and a careful family history may assist in arriving at that clinical judgment. Two families, for example, may present with similar dominant-submissive structures. One of the families may have been functioning at a more competent level months earlier, and the current dominant-submissive structure represents a regression in response to a stress, such as a serious illness in a family member. That finding suggests that this family may be much different from a family in which the same dominant-submissive structure has been characteristic of the family throughout its history.

Judgment regarding the level of family competence provides the clinician with an initial and tentative formulation which provides ideas about what treatment may be required. In some circumstances, for example when the family presents with a disturbed "identified" patient, an assessment of the family's level of competence may assist in the decision regarding whom to treat. At times, interventions at the level of the family are most productive, but in other situations intervention at the level of the individual holds more promise. Although the details of such clinical decisions are beyond the scope of this chapter, the family's level of competence may be one factor in formulating a comprehensive treatment plan.

We believe that the results of this study extend the applicability of this clinical tool to working-class black families by providing an empirical data base from which the clinician can plan interventions more confidently.

The Continuum of Family Competence is of use in the establishment of treatment goals because it predicts the changes associated with either positive or negative response by the family. Our clinical experience, for example, suggests that families move from chaotic to rigid structural alterations in response to successful family system interventions. In a like manner, families that present with rigid patterns of interaction (dominant-submissive or chronically conflicted) develop greater flexibility in response to helpful interventions. The impact of prolonged stress on the structure of families is in the opposite direction — that is, from flexibility to rigidity to chaos and, ultimately, to disintegration of the family. Although these observations come from clinical work rather than systematic research, such changes have theoretical validity. Recognition of what changes can be anticipated in family structure in response to treatment can be of considerable help in establishing both immediate and longer-term treatment goals. This study extends the range of clinical utility of the Continuum of Family Competence to working-class black families.

Clinicians use several, in some ways conflicting, approaches to the choice of specific techniques with which to intervene with dysfunctional families. One approach is "technique-centered"; that is, the clinician applies one approach with relatively slight variation to all families who present for help. This may reflect a belief in the overall therapeutic effectiveness of a particular technique, regardless of the family's structural pattern or level of function. The second approach is "family-centered" and strives to adopt approaches that are seen as appropriate to particular families at various levels of dysfunction. We favor the latter approach. Let us illustrate with the differences between two very different families presenting themselves for treatment. One family might come for help under circumstances of the stress of a significant loss. A previously flexible structure may be giving way, and a pattern of either escalating parental conflict or gradual dominance by one parent may be emerging. However, the clinician would find evidence of considerable strength within the family and consider family or marital therapy of a limited duration utilizing techniques that capitalize on family strengths.

The second family might come in response to the urging of others and present with one or more family members who are severely disabled from psychiatric disturbances. If the family structure is chaotic and there is no evidence of recent family regression, the clinician may consider a long-term commitment to family therapy in which he or she might have to become a functional part of the family and provide the family with structure, at times using interventions that are clearly authoritarian in nature. Under such circumstances the clinician is much less a consultant from the outside (as with the first family); rather, he or she becomes, for a time, an integral part of the family. His or her treatment might include assuming considerable control and power in order to provide the family with something other than a chaotic internal milieu, then gradually shifting that dominance to a member of the family.

These examples are at a very general level, and they are offered as illustrations only of the usefulness to the clinician of planning treatment on the basis of a formulation of the family's particular clinical situations within a theoretical framework derived from normative data. Of course, more could be said about the specific details of treatment techniques that have particular relevance for families at various levels of family competence. Such a discussion, however, is not pertinent to the point we wish to make: Dysfunctional families have a greater likelihood of being helped by clinicians who intervene with specific techniques appropriate to the realities of various families' particular situations.

However, a specific family's reality involves more than the family's level of competence and socioeconomic status. The ethnic identity of the family and its influence on family structure and process must be considered. It is often difficult to differentiate the impact of socioeconomic and ethnic variables. When socioeconomic factors are carefully controlled, measured differences in family interactional processes between ethnic groups tend to disappear.[13] Nevertheless, clinicians must be particularly sensitive to the role that ethnic factors may play in molding family life and, at the same time, not ascribe to ethnic variables that which evidence suggests are more likely the result of socioeconomic deprivation.

Minuchin and his colleagues call this fact to our attention in their classical study of the impact of family therapy on lower income, disorganized, minority families containing delinquent children.[14] They state that many signs of pathology which characterize some low-income families are present in a wide variety of families and there is "every reason" to believe that social class rather than ethnic variables plays the more important role. Recent contributions to the sparse literature on family therapy with black families, however, emphasize the need of the treating clinician to understand the importance of ethnic variables on family structure and function.

Pinderhughes also urges the clinician to understand the stresses impinging upon black families, because much of what appears to be family pathology may be efforts to deal with the victim system.[11] She stresses the importance of assessing the amount of support available in external systems, the degree to which the family's boundaries are flexible enough to use outside support, the congruence in role perception among family members, the degree of individuation in family members, and the presence of a stable balance of power within the family.

Hines and Boyd-Franklin[15] present the general outline of an "eco-structural"[16,17] approach to the treatment of black families. This approach is based on the understanding that "the black family" is in reality a heterogeneous group and the family therapist must be sensitive to the social, economic, and political realities of being "black" in this society. For lower-income families survival issues are paramount, and the family therapist must often serve as a system guide to help families learn more effectively how to deal with bureaucratic social service systems.

Hines and Boyd-Franklin direct their treatment suggestions to family therapists who deal with lower-income black families that are disorganized and often chaotic. They emphasize the importance of the time-limited, problem-solving, child-focused approaches. Family therapists can be most helpful through sensitivity to factors that are sustaining the problem rather than factors that played predisposing or precipitating roles. In this approach, however, the family therapist must understand that processes in the larger systems in which the family is embedded may be affecting the family's capacity to deal with the problem. A role that is directive and supportive is often the most helpful, and the family therapist needs to recognize and acknowledge the family's strengths as well as focusing on the problem or problems. Familiarity with the black culture can lead to a clearer understanding of communication processes that are idiosyncratic either to the black culture or to lower socioeconomic status.

Bagarozzi calls attention to the lack of clinical reports dealing with the treatment of black, middle-class families.[18] He emphasizes that generalizations drawn from investigations of lower-class black families are inappropriate for middle-class families, and family clinicians often have no reliable standard for understanding middle-class black families. The data he reviews suggest that middle-class black families have adopted mainstream American values but find their attainment more difficult because of racial discrimination. These social barriers to complete assimilation result in more extensive involvement in black church and kinship groups. Bagarozzi suggests that, although middle-class blacks are more like middle-class whites than they are like lower-class blacks, they remain a distinct ethnic subsociety. Black middle-class families differ from their white counterparts in three ways: The changes associated with the family life cycle may differ or be less clearly defined; family boundaries are more flexible; and the marital power structure is more likely egalitarian. Bagarozzi suggests that family therapists need to be particularly sensitive to the family's underlying anger and the ways it may be displaced to the family itself.

We believe that our study clearly suggests that clinicians who work with working-class black families should do so with the knowledge that, even under marginal socioeconomic circumstances, some such families are able to achieve patterns of relationships that are associated with both a strong sense of connectedness and high levels of individual autonomy. These families can tell us what is possible and, in so doing, assist clinicians in the establishment of appropriate treatment goals for families who need help.

AND, IN CONCLUSION

We do not want to close this report without returning to the families who let us enter their lives. Although most of the families reported that they learned something from their participation in the project, we wish to emphasize our debt to them. The families taught us a great deal; they demonstrated that, despite intense socioeconomic stress, high levels of family competence are possible. Mental health professionals need to understand more clearly the strengths that make this family competence a reality.

REFERENCES

1. Beavers, W. R. *Psychotherapy and growth: A family systems perspective.* New York: Brunner/Mazel, 1977.
2. Reiss, D. Families and the etiology of schizophrenia. Fishing: without a net. *Schizophrenia Bulletin,* Fall, 1975, *14,* 8–11.
3. Leff, J. P., & Vaughn, C. E. The interaction of life events and relatives' expressed emotion in schizophrenia and depressive neuroses. *British Journal of Psychiatry,* 1980, *136,* 146–153.
4. Vaughn, C. E., & Leff, J. P. The influence of family and social factors on the course of psychiatric illness. *British Journal of Psychiatry,* 1976, *129,* 125–137.
5. Vaughn, C. E., Snyder, K. S., Freeman, W., Jones, S., Falloon, I. R. H., & Liberman, R. P. Family factors in schizophrenic relapse: A replication. *Schizophrenia Bulletin,* 1982, *8*(2), 425–426.
6. Lewis, J. M., Beavers, W. R., Gossett, J. T., & Phillips, V. A. *No single thread: Psychological health in family systems.* New York: Brunner/Mazel, 1976.
7. Scanzoni, J. H. *The black family in modern society.* Boston: Allyn & Bacon, Inc., 1971.
8. Spiegel, J. An ecological model of ethnic families. In M. McGoldrick, J. K. Pearce, & J. Giordano (Eds.), *Ethnicity and family therapy.* New York: The Guilford Press, 1982.
9. Kluckhohn, C. Values and value orientation. In T. Parsons & E. Shils (Eds.), *Toward a general theory of action.* Cambridge, MA.: Harvard University Press, 1951.
10. Kluckhohn, F. R., & Strodtbeck, F. L. *Variations in value orientations.* Evanston, Ill.: Row, Peterson, 1961.
11. Pinderhughes, E. Afro-American families and the victim system. In M. McGoldrick, J. K. Pearce, J. Giordano (Eds.), *Ethnicity and family therapy.* New York: The Guilford Press, 1982.
12. Bowen, M. *Family therapy in clinical practice.* New York: Jason Aronson, 1978.

13. Henggeler, S. W., & Tavormina, J. B. Social class and race differences in family interaction: Pathological, normative, or confounding methodological factors? *Journal of Genetic Psychology,* 1980, *137,* 211-222.
14. Minuchin, S., Montalvo, B., Guerney, B. G., Jr., Rosman, B. L., & Schumer, F. *Familes of the slums.* New York: Basic Books, Inc., 1967.
15. Hines, P. M., & Boyd-Franklin, N. Black families. In M. McGoldrick, J. K. Pearce, J. Giordano (Eds.), *Ethnicity and family therapy.* New York: The Guilford Press, 1982.
16. Aponte, H. The family school interview: An ecostructural approach. *Family Process,* 1975, *15*(3), 303-311.
17. Aponte, H. Underorganization in the poor family. In P. Guerin (Ed.), *Family therapy: Theory and practice.* New York: Gardner Press, 1976.
18. Bagarozzi, D. A. Family therapy and the black middle class: A neglected area of study. *Journal of Marital and Family Therapy,* April, 1980, 159-166.

Beavers-Timberlawn Family Evaluation Scale

BEAVERS-TIMBERLAWN FAMILY EVALUATION SCALE

Rater......................................

Family Name......................................

Segment......................................

Date......................................

Instructions: The following scales were designed to assess the family functioning on continua representing interactional aspects of being a family. Therefore, it is important that you consider the entire range of each scale when you make your ratings. Please try to *respond on the basis of the videotape data alone*, scoring according to what you see and hear, rather than what you imagine might occur elsewhere.

I. *Structure of the Family*

A. Overt Power: Based on the entire tape, check the term that best describes your general impression of the overt power relationships of this family.

1	1.5	2	2.5	3	3.5	4	4.5	5
Chaos		Marked dominance		Moderate dominance		Led		Egalitarian
Leaderless; no one has enough power to structure the interaction.		Control is close to absolute. No negotiation; dominance and submission are the rule.		Control is close to absolute, Some negotiation, but dominance and submission are the rule.		Tendency toward dominance and submission, but most of the interaction is through respectful negotiation.		Leadership is shared between parents, changing with the nature of the interaction.

166

B. Parental Coalitions: Check the terms that best describe the relationship structure in this family.

1	1.5	2	2.5	3	3.5	4	4.5	5
Parent-child coalition				Weak parental coalition				Strong parental coalition

C. Closeness

1	1.5	2	2.5	3	3.5	4	4.5	5
Amorphous, vague and indistinct boundaries among members				Isolation, distancing				Closeness, with distinct boundaries among members

II. *Mythology:* Every family has a mythology; that is, a concept of how it functions as a group. Rate the degree to which this family's mythology seems congruent with reality.

1	1.5	2	2.5	3	3.5	4	4.5	5
Very congruent		Mostly congruent				Somewhat incongruent		Very incongruent

167

III. *Goal-Directed Negotiation:* Rate this family's overall efficiency in negotiating problem solutions.

1	1.5	2	2.5	3	3.5	4	4.5	5
Extremely efficient		Good				Poor		Extremely inefficient

IV. *Autonomy*

A. **Clarity of Expression:** Rate this family as to the clarity of disclosure of feelings and thoughts. This is not a rating of the intensity or variety of feelings, but rather of clarity of individual thoughts and feelings.

1	1.5	2	2.5	3	3.5	4	4.5	5
Very clear				Somewhat vague and hidden				Hardly anyone is ever clear

168

B. Responsibility: Rate the degree to which the family members take responsibility for their own past, present, and future actions.

1	1.5	2	2.5	3	3.5	4	4.5	5
Members regularly are able to voice responsibility for individual actions				Members sometimes voice responsibility for individual actions, but tactics also include sometimes blaming others, speaking in 3rd person or plural				Members rarely, if ever, voice responsibility for individual actions

C. Invasiveness: Rate the degree to which the members speak for one another, or make "mind reading" statements.

1	1.5	2	2.5	3	3.5	4	4.5	5
Many invasions				Occasional invasions				No evidence of invasions

D. Permeability: Rate the degree to which members are open, receptive and permeable to the statements of other family members.

1	1.5	2	2.5	3	3.5	4	4.5	5
Very open		Moderately open				Members frequently unreceptive		Members unreceptive

V. *Family Affect*

A. Range of Feelings:
Rate the degree to which this family system is characterized by a wide range expression of feelings.

1	1.5	2	2.5	3	3.5	4	4.5	5
Direct expression of a wide range of feelings		Direct expression of many feelings despite some difficulty		Obvious restriction in the expressions of some feelings		Although some feelings are expressed, there is masking of most feelings		Little or no expression of feelings

B. Mood and Tone:
Rate the feeling tone of this family's interaction.

1	1.5	2	2.5	3	3.5	4	4.5	5
Usually warm, affectionate, humorous and optimistic		Polite, without impressive warmth or affection; or frequently hostile with times of pleasure		Overtly hostile		Depressed		Cynical, hopeless and pessimistic

C. Unresolvable Conflict:
Rate the degree of seemingly unresolvable conflict.

1	1.5	2	2.5	3	3.5	4	4.5	5
Severe conflict, with severe impairment of group functioning		Definite conflict, with moderate impairment of group functioning		Definite conflict, with slight impairment of group functioning		Some evidence of unresolvable conflict, without impairment of group functioning		Little, or no unresolvable conflict

170

D. Empathy: Rate the degree of sensitivity to, and understanding of, each other's feelings within this family.

1	1.5	2	2.5	3	3.5	4	4.5	5
Consistent empathic responsiveness		For the most part, an empathic responsiveness with one another, despite obvious resistance		Attempted empathic involvement, but failed to maintain it		Absence of any empathic responsiveness		Grossly inappropriate responses to feelings

VI. *Global Health-Pathology Scale: Circle the number* of the point on the following scale that best describes this family's health or pathology.

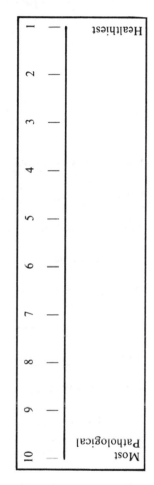

171

Demographic Interview

1. Name _____ 2. Telephone _____

3. Address _____

4. Husband's Occupation _____

5. Company _____

6. Title _____

7. Years Employed _____ 8. Telephone _____

9. Wife's Occupation _____

10. Company _____

11. Title _____

12. Years Employed _____ 13. Telephone _____

14. Family Income _____ Outside Income _____

15. Number of Marriages: Husband _____ Wife _____

16. Year of Current Marriage _____

17. Children   Age   Sex

_____

_____

_____

_____

_____

18. Any deaths in the immediate family? _____

_____

19. Do you own or rent your home? _____

20. Does anyone outside of the immediate family live in the home? ____

_____

21. Husband's Birth Place _____

22. Rural/City _____

23. Husband's Religious Affiliation _____

24. Husband's Educational Level _____

25. Wife's Birth Place _____

26. Rural/City _____

27. Wife's Religious Affiliation _____

28. Wife's Educational Level _____

Father's Original Family

Father

1. Birth Place _____

2. Educational Level _____

3. Occupation _____

4. Religious Affiliation _____

5. What is (was) your father like? _____

   _____

   _____

   _____

   _____

6. Would you say that your father tended to be pretty much of a perfectionist or was he more the happy-go-lucky type? _____

   _____

7. Would you say that your father usually looked for the best side of things
   (optimistic) or that he tended to see the worst side of things (pessimistic)?

   _____

8. Would you say that your father expressed his feelings (anger, elation, etc.)
   openly or did he pretty much keep his feelings to himself? _____

   _____

9. Do you have any brothers or sisters? _____

   Age: _____   Sex: _____

        _____   _____

        _____   _____

        _____   _____

Mother

10. Birth Place _____

11. Educational Level _____

12. Occupation _____

13. Religious Affiliation _____

14. What is (was) your mother like? _____

_____

_____

_____

_____

15. Would you say that your mother tended to be pretty much of a perfec-
    tionist or was she more the happy-go-lucky type? _____

    _____

16. Would you say that your mother usually looked for the best side of
    things (optimistic) or that she tended to see the worst side of things (pes-
    simistic)? _____

17. Would you say that your mother expressed her feelings (anger, elation,
    etc.) openly or did she pretty much keep her feelings to herself? _____

    _____

18. When you were growing up, who was in charge (ran things) at your house?

    _____

19. Which of your parents do (did) you feel closest to?

    _____

Current Individual Functioning

Father

A. Job Description
   1. What exactly does your work involve? What are your major respon-
      sibilities? Where do you work?

2. How many people are employed by you and/or responsible to you?
3. How much do you make (income)?
4. Has there been any recent change in your job, i.e., promotion, increase or decrease in responsibility?
5. If you could start all over again, would you choose the same occupation?
6. Regarding likes and dislikes of your job:
   a. What do you like best about your job?
   b. If you could change any aspect of your job, what changes would you make?
7. Do you have any other jobs?

B. Interests and Hobbies
   1. What are your interests and hobbies?
   2. Are you a member of any clubs or organizations?
   3. How else do you spend your day?

C. Usual Day
   1. Other than the fact that you are here for the interview today, has this been a more or less typical day for you; that is, has anything unusual happened recently that would make today somewhat unusual?

D. Losses
   1. Have you experienced any recent losses among family, friends, or people you work with; that is, have any of these people died, moved away, or somehow ended their relationship with you?

Mother's Original Family

Father

1. Birth Place _____

2. Educational Level _____

3. Occupation _____

4. Religious Affiliation _____

5. What is (was) your father like? _____

_____

_____

_____

_____ _____

_____

6. Would you say that your father tended to be pretty much of a perfectionist or was he more the happy-go-lucky type?

_____

7. Would you say that your father usually looked for the best side of things (optimistic) or that he tended to see the worst side of things (pessimistic)?

_____

8. Would you say that your father expressed his feelings (anger, elation, etc.) openly or did he pretty much keep his feelings to himself? _____

_____

9. Do you have any brothers or sisters? _____

Age: _____   Sex: _____

_____   _____

_____   _____

_____   _____

Mother

10. Birth Place _____

11. Educational Level _____

12. Occupation _____

13. Religious Affiliation _____

14. What is (was) your mother like? _____

_____

_____

_____

_____

_____

15. Would you say that your mother tended to be pretty much of a perfectionist or was she more the happy-go-lucky type? _____

_____

16. Would you say that your mother usually looked for the best side of things (optimistic) or that she tended to see the worst side of things (pessimistic)?

_____

17. Would you say that your mother expressed her feelings (anger, elation, etc.) openly or did she pretty much keep her feelings to herself?

_____

18. When you were growing up, who was in charge (ran things) at your house?

_____

19. Which of your parents do (did) you feel closest to? _____

Current Individual Functioning

A. Job Description
   1. Are you employed outside the home? If so, for how long? Do you want to work? Where do you work?
   2. What exactly does your work involve? What are your major responsibilities?
   3. How many people are employed by you and/or responsible to you? How many people are you responsible to?
   4. How much do you make (income)?

5. Has there been any recent change in your job, i.e., promotion, in- or decrease in responsibility?
6. If you could start over again, would you choose the same occupation? If the answer is no, what occupation would you choose?
7. Regarding the likes and dislikes or your job:
    a. What do you like best about your job?
    b. If you could change any aspect of your job, what change would you make?
8. Who helps you around the house?
9. Which of your household duties do you like the most? The least?

B. Interests and Hobbies
    1. What are your interests and hobbies?
    2. Are you a member of any clubs or organizations?
    3. How else do you spend your spare time?

C. Usual Day
    1. Other than the fact that you are here for the interview today, has this been a more or less typical day for you; that is, has anything unusual happened recently that would make today somewhat unusual?

D. Losses
    1. Have you experienced any recent losses among family, friends, or people you work with; that is, have any of these people died, moved away, or somehow ended their relationship with you?

Children

A. School
    1. What school do (did) you attend?
    2. What grade are you presently in (did you complete)?
    3. What kind of grades do you receive? Who helps you with your schoolwork?
    4. What is your favorite subject? What subject do you dislike the most?
    5. Are you involved in any extracurricular activities?

B. Job Description
    1. Are you employed outside of home? If so, for how long? Do you want to work? Where do you work?
    2. What exactly does your work involve? What are your major responsibilities?
    3. How many people are employed by you and/or responsible to you? How many people are you responsible to?

4. How much do you make (income)?

5. Has there been any recent change in your job, i.e., promotion, increase or decrease in responsibility?

6. If you could start over again, would you choose the same job? If the answer is no, what job would you choose?

7. Regarding likes and dislikes of your job:

   a. What do you like best about your job?

   b. If you could change any aspect of your job, what change would you make?

8. What do you do to help around the house?

9. Which of your household tasks do you like the most? The least?

B. Interests and Hobbies

   1. What are your interests and hobbies?

   2. Are you a member of any clubs or organizations?

   3. Outside of the time spent for the last two questions, how else do you spend your spare time?

C. Usual Day

   1. Other than the fact that you are here for the interview today, has this been a more or less typical day for you; that is, has anything unusual happened recently that would make today somewhat unusual?

D. Losses

   1. Have you experienced any recent losses among family, friends, or people you work with; that is, have any of these people, died, moved away, or somehow ended their relationship with you?

Family Medical History

We are interested in the past medical history of the family. As such, we need to obtain as much information as possible in order to develop an estimate of family medical health. For these purposes, date the onset of the family medical history to the parental marriage.

1. *Serious Illness* — Has any member of the family experienced a serious (life-threatening) illness? If so, please give details.

2. *Hospitalization* — Please list all hospitalizations for each member of the family (exclude childbirth). We are interested in the cause of hospitalization,

month and year in which it occurred, and approximate length of hospitalization.

3. *Serious Accidents* — Has any member of the family experienced a serious accident? If so, please give details.

4. *Have there been any miscarriages, stillbirths or neonatal deaths?* If so, please give approximate date and brief description of the circumstances.

5. *Presence of Medical Conditions* — We are interested in all chronic medical conditions which either require medical supervision or medication, or interfere with family members' productivity or activity or efficiency. Please include the full spectrum of conditions from those more serious ailments like heart disease or peptic ulcer to those less serious like sinusitis or indigestion for each family member.

Father —

Mother —

Child 1 —

Child 2 —

Child 3 —

Child 4 —

6. *Interference with Usual Pursuits*—We are interested in your estimate of the number of days each member of the family was unable to work, go to school, or tend to usual responsibilities because of illness or accidents *during the past year*. Please check the number of days which most closely describes the total time lost for each family member.

	None	Less than 5 days	5–10 days	More than 10 days
Father	_____	_____	_____	_____
Mother	_____	_____	_____	_____
Child 1	_____	_____	_____	_____
Child 2	_____	_____	_____	_____
Child 3	_____	_____	_____	_____
Child 4	_____	_____	_____	_____

7. *Nature of Health Care*—Here we are interested in a number of issues. Please check the box which most closely describes your family.

	True	False
a. We have a family doctor.	_____	_____
b. We have periodic checkups.	_____	_____
c. We consult physicians only when ill.	_____	_____
d. We have a pediatrician.	_____	_____
e. We are exacting about inoculations, boosters, etc.	_____	_____
f. We have periodic dental examinations.	_____	_____

8. *Medications*—Here we are interested in the medication each family member takes. These would run the range from aspirin to antacids to tranquilizers to digitalis. Please record all medication use *during the past month* for each family member.

	Medication	*Symptoms*	*Frequency*
Father			
Mother			
Child 1			
Child 2			
Child 3			
Child 4			

9. *Estimate of Family Health*—Please check the statement which most closely describes each family member's general health status.

	Usually Healthy	Average Healthy	Slightly Unhealthy	Distinctly Unhealthy
Father	_____	_____	_____	_____

	Usually Healthy	Average Healthy	Slightly Unhealthy	Distinctly Unhealthy
Mother	_____	_____	_____	_____
Child 1	_____	_____	_____	_____
Child 2	_____	_____	_____	_____
Child 3	_____	_____	_____	_____
Child 4	_____	_____	_____	_____

10. *Response to Illness* — Some individuals respond to medical illness with a type of refusal to "give in" to the symptoms while others do not respond in that manner. Please indicate by number your estimate of each family member's typical response to an illness.
    1. Tends to deny illness and pushes on.
    2. Reacts with appropriate response of bed rest, medicine, etc.
    3. Is somewhat quick to call the doctor, go to bed, etc.
    4. Obviously capitalizes on symptoms with exaggerated response.

Father ____ Mother ____ Child 1 ____ Child 2 ____ Child 3 ____

Child 4 _____

11. *Family's Recent Emotional Losses* — We are interested in an estimate of the important or significant losses experienced by the family *during the past two years.* Here include family members, friends, and relatives who have died, moved away, or in some way become alienated from the family during that two-year period. For each loss, we would like the family's estimate of who in the family experienced the loss most intensely or "took it the hardest."

Family Characteristics Inventory

Name _____

Date _____

The following statements fit some families better than others. Please circle the number that best describes how well each statement fits your family.

	Does Not Fit Our Family At All	Fits Our Family Some	Fits Our Family Very Well		
1. We live in a good neighborhood.	1	2	3	4	5
2. Our family talks things out.	1	2	3	4	5
3. We have a sense of humor.	1	2	3	4	5
4. There is an opportunity for each member to express himself in his own way.	1	2	3	4	5
5. There are activities which we all enjoy doing together.	1	2	3	4	5
6. We respect each other's feelings.	1	2	3	4	5
7. In our home, we feel loved.	1	2	3	4	5
8. We have the right kinds of friends.	1	2	3	4	5
9. Life is exciting most of the time for our family.	1	2	3	4	5

	Does Not Fit Our Family At All		Fits Our Family Some		Fits Our Family Very Well
10. Discipline is moderate and consistent.	1	2	3	4	5
11. Educational goals are important to us.	1	2	3	4	5
12. There is a sense of belonging in our family.	1	2	3	4	5
13. Our family is a reliable, dependable family.	1	2	3	4	5
14. We establish reasonable goals for ourselves.	1	2	3	4	5
15. We encourage development of potential in all members of our family.	1	2	3	4	5
16. Our family is a happy one.	1	2	3	4	5
17. The future looks good to our family.	1	2	3	4	5
18. Our family members have good friends.	1	2	3	4	5
19. Understanding and sympathy come easy in our family.	1	2	3	4	5
20. We have many outside interests and activities.	1	2	3	4	5
21. One or more of our family members is odd.	1	2	3	4	5
22. Our family needs no one outside to make us happy.	1	2	3	4	5
23. Our family expects a lot from its members.	1	2	3	4	5
24. We trust each other.	1	2	3	4	5
25. In our family children obey parents.	1	2	3	4	5
26. Children in our family are treated fairly.	1	2	3	4	5
27. Members of our family continually grumble about work they do for the family.	1	2	3	4	5
28. There is frequent laughter in our family.	1	2	3	4	5
29. Our family follows examples set by other families.	1	2	3	4	5
30. We have well understood but unspoken rules concerning family behavior.	1	2	3	4	5
31. Members fear to express their real opinions.	1	2	3	4	5

	Does Not Fit Our Family At All	Fits Our Family Some	Fits Our Family Very Well
32. Only certain kinds of ideas may be ex-pressed.	1	2 3	4 5
33. There is strict discipline.	1	2 3	4 5
34. We just cannot tell each other our real feelings.	1	2 3	4 5
35. Good manners and proper behavior are very important to us.	1	2 3	4 5
36. We do not talk about sex.	1	2 3	4 5
37. We have very good times together.	1	2 3	4 5
38. We can get mad at each other but it doesn't last long.	1	2 3	4 5
39. We need each other.	1	2 3	4 5
40. We are a strong, competent family.	1	2 3	4 5
41. We are satisfied with the way we now live.	1	2 3	4 5
42. We forgive each other easily.	1	2 3	4 5
43. We can adjust well to new situations.	1	2 3	4 5
44. We are not as happy as I would like.	1	2 3	4 5
45. Each of us tries to be the kind of person the others will like.	1	2 3	4 5
46. There are serious differences in our standards and values.	1	2 3	4 5
47. We accept each other's friends.	1	2 3	4 5
48. Each member has a job to do.	1	2 3	4 5
49. Our family life follows a regular schedule.	1	2 3	4 5
50. We like to get together with relatives.	1	2 3	4 5

Global Life Adaptation Scale

Interview # _____

Rater _____

Date _____

Please score the individual's life adaptation as judged by his or her ability to work, love, and play. Work can be judged by the quality of functioning in employment, school, or the maintenance of a home. Evidence for the ability to love may be elicited from the individual's ability to: 1) maintain friendships; 2) establish constructive relationships with family members; and 3) establish intimate relationships. Evidence of the ability to play may be assessed by the individual's pleasurable, nondestructive participation in leisure-time activities. Evidence of psychiatric symptomatology may be grounds for lowering the overall score. Please integrate your assessment of the individual's functioning in these areas into a rating of life adaptation.

1	2	3	4	5
Poor		Average		Superior

Check if data are insufficient to arrive at an evaluation _____

Index

MAY 1 0 1984

NOV 2 4 1985

1 2 1987

DEC 1 2 1987

NOV 1 3 1989

DEC 1 4 1989

DEC 1 1 1990

APR 1 7 1991

DEC 0 2 1991